THE ARCHITECTURAL RECORD BOOK OF VACATION HOUSES, SECOND EDITION

the ARCHITECTURAL RECORD book of vacation houses

second edition

Selected by the editors of Architectural Record

An Architectural Record Book McGraw-Hill Book Company

NEW YORK
ST. LOUIS
SAN FRANCISCO
AUCKLAND
BOGOTÁ
DÜSSELDORF
JOHANNESBURG
LONDON
MADRID
MEXICO
MONTREAL
NEW DELHI
PANAMA
PARIS
SÃO PAULO
SINGAPORE
SYDNEY
TOKYO
TORONTO

The editors for this book were Jeremy Robinson and Martin Filler.
The designer was Jan V. White.
The production editor was Patricia Mintz.

The book was set in Optima by Monotype Composition Company, Inc.
Printed by Halliday Lithograph Corporation
and bound by The Book Press.

Library of Congress Cataloging in Publication Data
Main entry under title:
The Architectural record book of vacation houses.

   "An Architectural record book."
   Includes index.
   1. Summer houses.   2. Architecture, Domestic—
Designs and plans.   I. Architectural record.
NA7574.A7 1977   728'.7   77-3332
ISBN 0-07-002337-9

■ 34567890 HDHD   78654321098■

Contents

Preface

The sixty-two houses presented in this second edition cover the most recent trends in vacation house design since the first edition was published in 1970. The major crosscurrents of house design in the years this book covers are well represented here. The emerging "factions" of high-style architecture—the "Whites" (exemplified by such firms as Gwathmey-Siegel) versus the "Greys" (represented by the old MLTW firm and the work of two of its principals, Charles Moore and William Turnbull)—are discussed as well as the work of architects whose work is known only within a small vacation community, such as Earl Burns Combs and Robert L. Rotner.

These vacation houses are as varied as the design philosophies of their architects and the bank accounts of their owners. They span the continent—from New York to California, with stops along the way in Michigan, Minnesota, Nebraska and Colorado. Grouped into five chapters by virtue of their sites (which in themselves determine to some extent how houses look and function), the individual natures of the houses are underscored by the fact that each was custom-designed by an architect with the needs and desires of a specific family in mind. But although these houses are very personal solutions to very personal programs, they contain a wealth of specific ideas applicable to other vacation houses, houses which might differ in every other aspect.

This, frankly, is a dream book, one which will be most successful only if it encourages its readers to use this as a jumping-off point for thinking about the places in which they live—or those in which they would like to live some day. *Architectural Record,* in whose pages these houses originally appeared, has since 1956 sponsored the annual "Record Houses" awards program honoring the most outstanding examples of contemporary house design completed in the preceding year. Of the sixty-two houses collected here, forty-three were Record Houses of the Year. Some of the houses, since their original publication in *Architectural Record*, have become classics of sorts, while others, like Robert A. M. Stern's and John S. Hagmann's house on eastern Long Island, have already done much to further the reputations of their architects. But for the most part, these houses have been fulfilling the purposes for which they were built: to provide an enjoyable, relaxing, and above all, refreshing change from the ways in which their owners live in their year-round houses.

The United States Department of Commerce reports that there are almost two million second homes in this country, two-thirds of which are located in the Northeast and North Central regions of the country. The large-scale population shifts that have been reported toward the so-called "Sun Belt" regions in the United States might well affect that distribution in the near future. Sixty per cent of all American vacation homes are within 100 miles of their owner's principal residence, and 80% are within a 200 mile radius. Other characteristics of the vacation house owner include the likelihood of relative affluence (80% of vacation house owners also own their first home) and of maturity (most second-home owners no longer have children at home, and 20% are over sixty-five years old). As for the houses themselves, the U.S. government surveys show that most (60%) vacation houses are used only seasonally, with the remainder being used throughout the year. Once again, this is a function of the location of many vacation houses, which are frequently located in areas made inaccessible during bad weather, and by methods of construction, which sometimes do not provide for year-round living.

The recession in the construction industry has affected residential building least of any other building type, the theory being that basic shelter will always be needed, while a new school or museum can be done without. But vacation house activity has been affected by other factors as well: increasing governmental regulation and environmental activism in resort areas are growing each year. The recent energy crisis still lingers as a potential problem to owning property accessible only by private transportation. And the spiraling inflation of recent years has been leaving fewer discretionary dollars for Americans to deal with. Despite these difficulties, though, it can be said that the vacation house market is certainly surviving. Three basic reasons for this include the fact that those in the economic bracket that could have afforded a vacation house were never in the marginal income group which inflation has eliminated as potential second-home owners. Second, those who can still afford a vacation house are perhaps more likely to want one now precisely because of those same inflationary trends: realizing that home-ownership is one of the soundest hedges against inflation, and that building costs, in any event, are unlikely ever to become cheaper. And finally, as the demographic profile of the second-home buyer would indicate, many early-middle-aged owners have planned their vacation homes to serve eventually as retirement homes. New kinds of financing arrangements and other cost-cutting concepts (such as the "time-sharing" concept) are clear indications of the survival of the vacation house concept in light of general conditions that would have seemed to dim the future of the second home.

Examination of the sixty-two houses in this book will give the *real* answer for the likely survival of the second home as a part of the American Dream. The natural beauties of America are underscored by these houses, places where their owners can retreat to be brought back into contact with the Nature which eludes us in our cities. The Sea Ranch in California is perhaps the best example of the phenomenon. Situated on the Pacific coast 100 miles north of San Francisco, this large second-home community has been one of the most successful efforts of its kind, economically, architecturally and ecologically. Its site-planning, landscaping and architecture have already won numerous prizes and international recognition. Its rugged beauty is strictly protected to ensure the preservation of its still-unspoiled site, and it has become a model of intelligent and ecologically sound development. Since its development has been limited by predetermined goals, it cannot appeal to the "herding instinct" that has ruined so many resort communities in the past. It is not serviced by superhighways, and travel in the winter, over treacherous, winding mountain highways, can be hazardous. But still, it (and several imitations up and down the coast) have become increasingly desirable vacation areas for just these reasons. The protection of the vacation site itself is what holds such strong appeal, and it is that same appeal, which draws millions of Americans towards vacation houses each year, that seems the most likely to ensure the future of houses like these.

The houses here show the very best ideas for living a relaxed and uncomplicated life away from the pressures of our increasingly urbanized society. "Let's get away from it all," goes the refrain from the old song, and here are over five dozen new and exciting ways of how to do it.

Thirteen

resort and country houses

1:

Husband and wife architects Richard and Judith Newman designed this remarkable summer house for themselves and their children on a corner lot in Saltaire, Fire Island, New York. The scrub pine that grows so thickly on the site masks the elevations and provides a dense curtain of privacy—especially on the lower levels of the house where tufted greenery feels almost like an interior finish.

The square, 32- by 32-foot plan is complicated by seven distinct interior levels. The desirable functional separations that result (see plan) provide a lively volumetric flow that invites rather than inhibits movement throughout the house. As a reflection of the Newman's informal summer lifestyle, the kitchen/dining space occupies a prime location in the spatial hierarchy as it overlooks major living spaces and opens across a narrow deck to long views of island and water. Another unusual feature of the house is a double-height, screened portico with a deliberately ambiguous indoor/outdoor character that encloses several trees and provides overflow play space.

Most furniture in the house is built in—a design imperative for this island site. Finishes have been omitted where they are not necessary. The house has no soffits or ceilings. Where finishes are required, they have been selected for their durability. The detailing has an agreeable simplicity throughout. Yet the results are anything but spartan. The Newman house is colorful, comfortable, inventive, carefully sited (the builder tied back trees to apply exterior siding) and most important of all—fun. Like the trees it has captured, the Newman house has made happy captives of its owners who spend every moment they can in their ingratiating new surroundings.

UPPER LEVELS

LOWER LEVELS

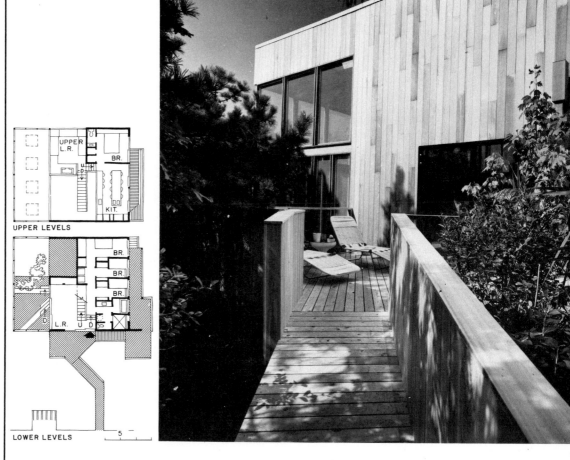

NEWMAN HOUSE, Fire Island, New York, Architects and owners: *Richard and Judith Newman.* Structural engineer: *J. Ames.* Contractor: *Joseph Chasas;* Photographer: *William Maris.*

In keeping with the rough, unfinished character of the house, the Newmans have used open shelving for a wide variety of storage requirements. With generous openings on all elevations, the house makes the most of summer breezes from any quarter—an obvious virtue on this Fire Island site.

Quarry tile, used on counters, is one of the few indulgences.

The double-height, screened portico with its hostage trees opens to the upper living room through a sliding window assembly for ventilation as well as for supervision of children's play.

Trees receive almost as much daylight now as they did before.

2:

Norman Jaffe's houses belong to that Romantic stream in American building that is lyrical and frankly idiosyncratic—that stream that seeks its formal inspiration in images stored up and reconstructed from the remembered past. The images, sometimes drawn from film, are as varied as human experience allows. These images may be his own or his clients, usually a compound of both, but they nearly always include elements of fantasy— elements that are blended and necessarily blurred in the translation into building. Even in blurred form, though, their presence is felt to the extent that each house in this portfolio has a substantially different look, tempo and formal idiom. But where there are differences, there are also striking similarities. Jaffe's houses nearly always respond sympathetically to their sites. They almost always celebrate a sense of shelter that finds expression in powerful roof forms with deep, overhanging eaves, sometimes reaching down to grade. And, all show signs of the familiar struggle between formal concerns and the routine requirements of day-to-day living.

"Long, flat planes of cedar, cantilevered over a stone base" is the phrase Jaffe uses to describe the fundamental concept of this house he designed for the Marvin Schlacters on a flat site in Bridgehampton, Long Island. Here, the ground has been carefully prepared to receive the house. Its mild undulations have been augmented to contrast with the sharp-edged, severely horizontal volumes of the house and to make the ground plane an integral part of the whole composition.

The stone is laid up in natural cleavage with mortarless top courses held only by the bermed earth surrounding them. The glazing line is set back and protected by the deep overhangs of the cedar-clad superstructure. The gravel of the driveway is an apron leading right to the front door.

Inside, the space flows effortlessly through a combination of low- and high-ceilinged areas culminating in the living-dining space (photo page 8). Rich, high-contrast finishes and simple but expressive details give the Schlacter house an elegant, voluptuous quality that excites the eye and stimulates the senses.

SCHLACTER HOUSE, Long Island, New York. Architect: *Norman Jaffe—Mark Matthews, job captain.* Contractor: *M.S. Construction Company.*

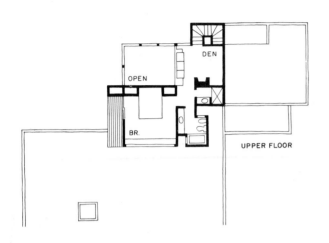

UPPER FLOOR

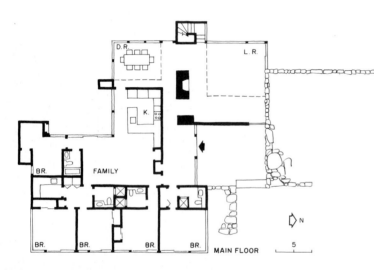

MAIN FLOOR   5

3:

STOR. · OPEN · BR.

GALLERY

OPEN · REC.

BUNK

STOR. · BR.

SECOND LEVEL

BR.

OPEN

STUDY

FOURTH LEVEL

U · STOR.

STUDIO · STUDY

FIRST LEVEL · 5

KIT.

OPEN

PIT · L.R. · D.R.

THIRD LEVEL

The architect's own house and studio in Bridgehampton is a synthesis of the wood shingles, steeply-pitched roofs, dormers and chimneys that traditionally characterize regional houses in eastern Long Island. Though exaggerating these features in scale, the house stops safely short of burlesquing them, for nowhere are the functions of the house compromised by these exaggerations.

Stepping up under the roof at the intermediate levels are a complex series of spaces, Piranesian in conception and thrust, which house the regular range of domestic spaces. Under these, but not pressed down by them, is the architect's studio (next pages), a double-height space filled with daylight from several sources. The uppermost level houses a master bedroom, bath and small study, from which the spatial composition is most fully revealed (photo left). The massive chimney includes a large skylight that brings daylight deep into the house.

Throughout the interiors, wood is used skillfully in ways that exploit its potential for warmth, color and pattern.

JAFFE HOUSE, Bridgehampton, Long Island, New York. Architect and contractor: *Norman Jaffe.*

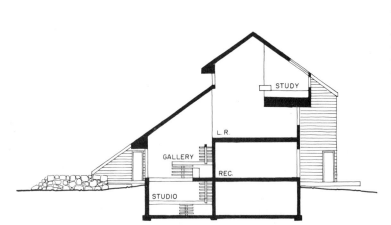

Interior walls of the Jaffe house are finished in cypress. Floors are Pennsylvania slate and pine. Major openings face east and west. The north and south elevations have limited exposures for high contrast and strong exterior shadows.

4:

A central court, with sub-spaces that pinwheel around an existing sycamore, is the primary design feature in this Long Island residence by architect Hobart Betts. This outdoor space is decked in cedar, canopied by tree branches, and enclosed by the major elements of the house. Living, dining, kitchen and master bedroom functions are enclosed in the L-shaped, shed-roofed structure on the north side and form a self-sufficient series of spaces when the owners are alone. Two guest bedrooms and a bath share the western side, and garage and storage complete the plan to the east (see plan).

Because the house is sited on a flat lot of modest size with no compelling views and surrounded by neighboring houses, Betts settled on the court design and placed all major openings to the inside. This introversion insures privacy for owners and guests while providing its users with an exceptionally pleasant outdoor space for entertaining on almost any scale.

Internal circulation is organized around the court and defined overhead by low, flat ceilings—a design device that heightens the sense of transition between inside and out and also offers a dramatic contrast to the high-ceilinged living, dining and sleeping spaces.

Betts has elected to relate this house to its two-story, neo-colonial neighbors by expressing the exterior walls as a continuous plane wrapping around four sides and interrupted only where necessary to provide access to the central court. At these points (photo opposite top) the deck extends outward in the form of a tongue. The elevations conceal the degree of fragmentation inherent in the plan but preserve an important sense of unity. Inside, this unity is achieved by a careful shaping of the spaces and a marvellously consistent use of materials, textures and finishes.

PRIVATE RESIDENCE, Eastern Long Island. Architects: *Hobart Betts Associates—Moulton Andrus, project architect.* Structural engineer: *Stanley Gleit.* Contractor: *Ralph L. Otis.*

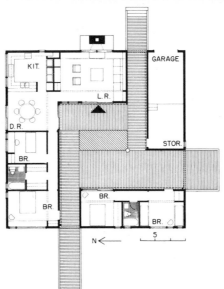

Maris-Semel photos

KIT.

GARAGE

L.R.

D.R.

STOR.

BR.

BR.

BR.

BR.

N ←   5

Construction is platform wood framing. Interior and exterior wall surfaces are rough-sawn cedar siding applied vertically throughout. Floors are white oak stained dark. Painted wood trim and cabinets contrast brightly with the rough-sawn cedar.

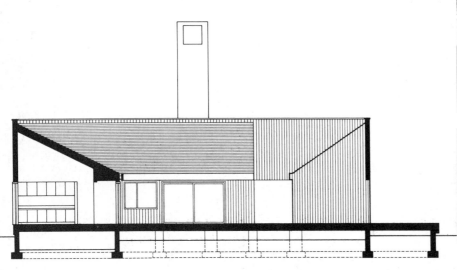

Maris-Semel photos

The corner condition, created by the intersection of tilted roof planes over the kitchen (photo right) has been handled with skill. The cabinet partition next to the dining table is kept away from the ceiling while the partition between kitchen and living room reaches full height to provide support for the dropped ceiling over the circulation space as it turns the corner.

5:

Here, on a softly sloping Vermont hillside, is a summer and winter weekend house for an active family of seven. Reached by an access road through a thick mask of trees, the house is set in a clearing on the crest of the hill at a point where woodlands give way to meadow. A low stone wall, just south of the house, emphasizes this division. From their living room, the owners can feel the shroud of trees about them but look beyond the wall to long, unobstructed views of surrounding country. At right angles to the main living spaces, and separated by a strip of deck, is a second smaller structure that contains a garage and recreation space. The void between the two structures provides an arrival point and offers entry to either building.

The main spaces of the house are tightly organized around a massive chimney breast. Living, kitchen and dining spaces are carved out of one large volume with separations suggested by built-in counters and changes in ceiling height. Bedrooms, separated by baths, complete the first floor plan. Upstairs, three bunkrooms, each containing four beds, are spaced out by baths in a pattern that offers both privacy and economy. Bands of clerestories bring light into the top of the house and illuminate the upper level corridor.

The forms of the house are reminiscent of Vermont's farm buildings built in a combination platform and post-and-beam framing system. The exterior walls are vertical cedar boarding stained to a silver gray. Interior partitions and ceilings are finished in cedar boards left natural. Doors, cabinetwork, fireplace and chimney are painted white.

PRIVATE RESIDENCE, Southern Vermont. Architect: *Hobart Betts—Roger Lang, project architect.* Engineers: *Gleit, Olenek & Associates* (structural). Landscape architect: *Terrence Boyle.* Contractor: *MacDonald & Swan Construction.* Photographer: *George Cserna.*

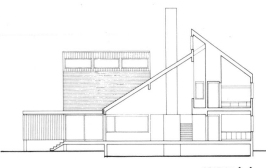

SECTION A-A

STOR.   BR.

UPPER PART OF L.R.

BR.

SAUNA

SECOND FLOOR

GARAGE

PLAYROOM

BR.

L.R.

KIT.

D.R.

A   A

FIRST FLOOR   0   5   10 FT.

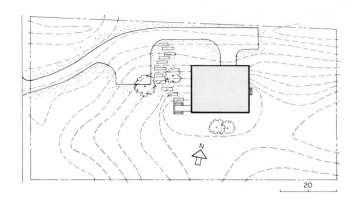

6:

Robert L. Rotner

Architect Rotner's client for this house was Robert Leader, who built it on a lot adjoining his own house to protect the view. Like the Burke house, the cost was kept to approximately $21 per square foot and the total came to $41,200.

The object was to design a house that could meet the non-specialized requirements of the small family or couple seeking a vacation house. No special built-ins were called for. The rooms were to be conventionally shaped and easy to furnish with basic pieces. In brief, what was wanted was a house without idiosyncracies—a "sensible" house. One last requirement was that the house be kept as low as possible, so it wouldn't impinge upon Leader's vision. How to build such a house on a small budget, within the modern idiom, and still give it character?

Rotner used the simplest means available to him. He put the dining room, kitchen and three bedrooms all on one level, three steps above the living room, tucking the garage under the bedroom wing. The living room is a pleasant shape, with a carefully studied ratio of wall space to window allowing easy and straightforward placement of furniture. Throughout the house the placement of windows and doors allows the rooms to be furnished without special problems.

In orienting the house and in the placement of decks, much attention was given to light. The living room faces north opening upon a deck, with windows to the west as well. The entrance porch is to the south (opposite page, top), and a deck serving all three bedrooms is to the east (above left). On sunny mornings this deck is ideal for breakfast.

As in the Burke house, costs were pared by using single-layer wood frame construction, grooved plywood sheets being used on the exterior. Unlike the other three houses, however, the exterior finish was not carried indoors, wall board painted white being used instead. Other

Robert L. Rotner

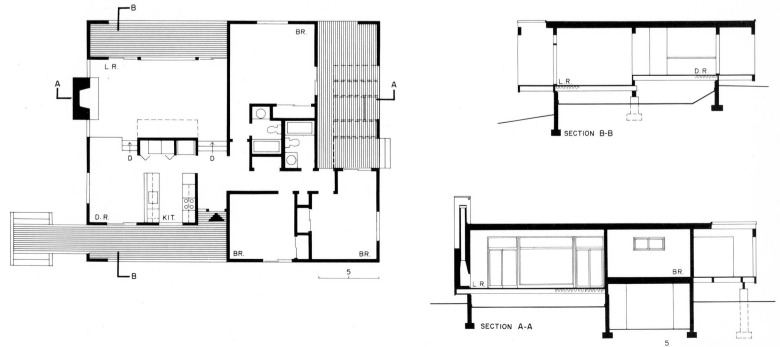

SECTION B-B

SECTION A-A

5

LEADER HOUSE, Sag Harbor, New York. Owner: *Robert Leader*. Architect and Photographer: *Robert L. Rotner*. Structural Engineer: *N. H. Bettigole*. Construction: *Sag Hill Builders*.

economies include standard windows and a prefabricated fireplace and chimney.

Although the furniture in the living room (above) is temporary, and the angle from which the photograph was taken makes the room appear narrower than it is, it can be seen as a simple, carefully detailed and comfortable space. The skylight which illuminates the continuous wall will enhance the room regardless of how it will be furnished in the future. The steps just visible at the rear of the photo lead to the small dining area (right). This space has also been studied with care. The window and dining room table belong together, as they do in all carefully worked out houses. Since this window faces west, early summer evening meals can be enjoyed in the setting sun.

Although at the time the house was completed, it was a buyer's rather than a seller's market, up until the time he finally sold it Leader received a number of good offers attesting to the appeal of the house.

James Brett

7: **C**lient Sol de Swaan owns a full acre site in the rapidly disappearing Bridgehampton, Long Island potato fields. Although it doesn't front on the ocean, it has an ocean view. De Swaan's budget was $55,000 and his house cost approximately $26 per square foot in 1972-73. It is almost identical in size and materials to the Robert Leader house, but quite different spatially, because of differences in family requirements and site.

Unlike the Leader and Burke houses which are bachelor residences primarily, although they can be transformed for family use, the de Swaan house was designed from the beginning for a young family with one child. And unlike the Leader house, which is hidden in the woods, the de Swaan house is highly visible from all four sides and demands by its placement to be treated as a work of sculpture in the round. As such, it is highly successful, even though basically it is merely a humble box as the photo indicates.

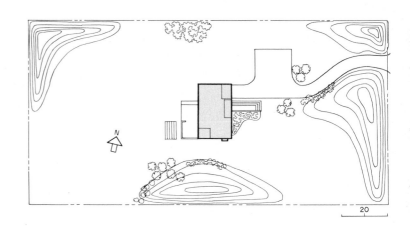

The view from the living room is to the rear, over the potato fields and the terrace deck is located on this side. The house has four additional decks—one at the entrance and three which adjoin upstairs bedrooms. Each deck has several exposures and two overlook the ocean; all are partially shaded.

The garage is at grade and four steps above is the living-dining and utility area. Bedrooms, bathrooms, storage and decks occupy the remaining two levels as can be seen in the plans and sections.

The house is finished with red cedar tongue and groove siding over plywood sheathing on the exterior and the identical siding is used throughout the interiors. In all of his houses, architect Rotner uses standard metal kitchen cabinets framed in wood giving his kitchen installations a custom look. The interior furnishings of this house were selected by the architect. The contractor was Sag Hill Builders, Inc.

Mildred F. Schmertz

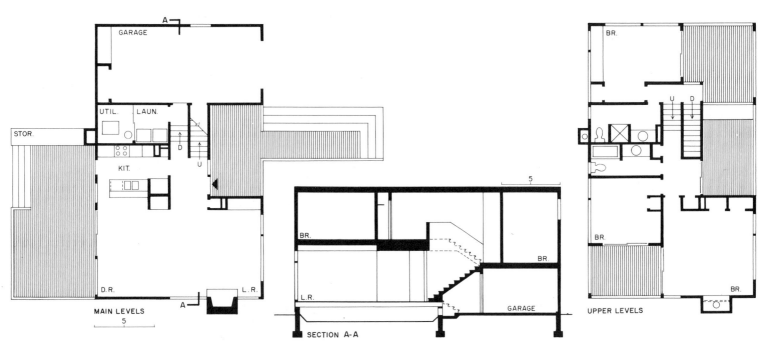

GARAGE

A

STOR.

UTIL.   LAUN.

KIT.

D.R.   L.R.

A

MAIN LEVELS

5

BR.

L.R.   GARAGE

SECTION A-A

5

BR.

U   D

BR.

BR.

UPPER LEVELS

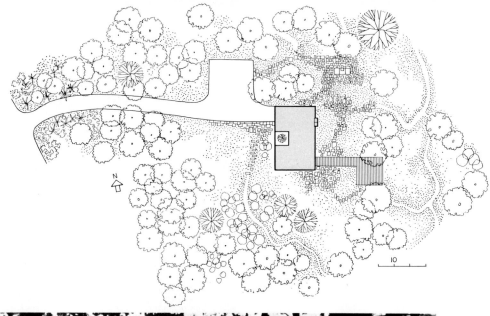

8:

Robert L. Rotner

Architect Rotner's client, Robert Leader, wanted to sit on his terrace in the early evening and gaze upon the church spires of the village. At night he hoped to see the lights of the town. His heavily wooded site, however, offered no vistas, and it soon became clear that the living quarters of the house should perch in the treetops. To find the best elevation for town viewing, Rotner and Leader climbed a few trees and decided the higher the better.

To achieve as much elevation as possible, the house was designed on four levels as the section indicates. Five steps down from the entrance level are the bedrooms and garage and eleven steps up are the kitchen-dining area and the library. Opening off the dining area is a bridge leading to a small dining terrace (opposite page, right). At the top of the last flight of stairs is the living room which at one end overlooks the kitchen so that the owner, who cooks, remains in touch with his guests. From the master bedroom at grade, a path leads to

a gazebo roofed by the dining terrace.

The house has been designed for a bachelor with resale value in mind. It is essentially a three-bedroom, two-bathroom house suitable for a small family, but the bedrooms are so located that one serves Leader conveniently as a combined library and guest bedroom and the other as a combined office and guest bedroom.

The scheme provides a lot of privacy for a house so small. The sleeping areas are neither underneath nor adjacent to the living room, allowing those who choose peace and quiet to get away from a party. The extended porch with gazebo below economically increases the dimensions of the house and intensifies its relationship to the outdoors.

The house is of wood frame construction with tongue and groove cedar on plywood sheathing. It was built by Hal Young General Construction Co. for approximately $26 per square foot in 1970-71, for a total of $52,000.

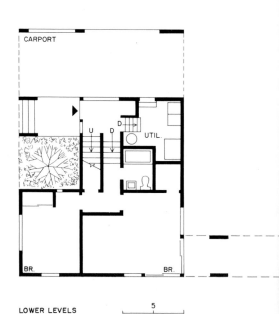

CARPORT

UTIL.

BR.   BR.

LOWER LEVELS   5

James Brett photos except where noted

Robert L. Rotner

Robert L. Rotner

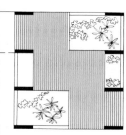

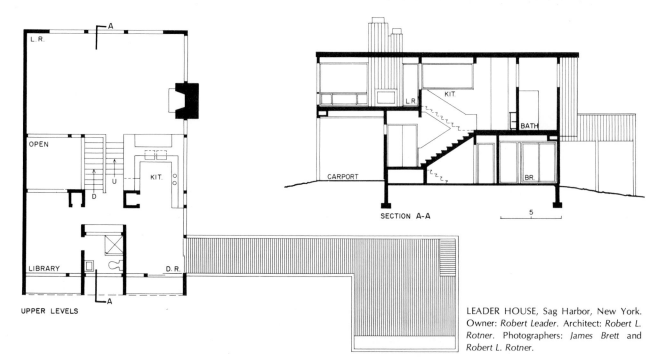

UPPER LEVELS

L.R.

OPEN

KIT.

U

D

LIBRARY

D.R.

SECTION A-A

5

L.R.

KIT.

BATH

CARPORT

BR.

LEADER HOUSE, Sag Harbor, New York. Owner: *Robert Leader*. Architect: *Robert L. Rotner*. Photographers: *James Brett* and *Robert L. Rotner*.

9:

Its cedar siding stained green to blend with the leaves of a surrounding forest, this house—designed by architect Peter Bohlin for his parents—is in fine sympathy with a natural site of 18 acres in Cornwall, Connecticut. Seemingly modest from the approach (photo overleaf, top), the building is actually a carefully studied progression of vertically expanding spaces, which lead the visitor from the dark shade of evergreen trees at the drive and entry bridge into the high living room with a view of dappled sunlight through lacy deciduous branches.

An industrial-type light standard on the parking-lot side of the bridge begins a series of vertical, rust-red-painted orientation points in the visitor's progress. Others are the surrounds of the glazed front door, those round exposed-concrete columns that extend through the interior and—finally—the industrial-type framing of the living room windows expose the climactic view. The route over the bridge leads past the end of the building, which is only 12 feet wide, under the low roof of the porch, and down several flights of stairs until the full height of the living room is reached.

Careful attention to detail has made a dramatic product of simple materials such as corrugated aluminum for roofing, tongue-and-groove siding and circular concrete piers. Bohlin states that the contrast between large sheets of glass in the standard, black-finished sliding doors and the small panes of glass elsewhere (also standard) is intentional.

Costs for the 1,800-square-foot structure were just over $30 per foot. The project has won two awards for design.

Architects: Bohlin and Powell
  partner-in-charge:
  Peter Bohlin
  project architect:
  Russell Roberts
  182 North Franklin Street
  Wilkes-Barre, Pennsylvania and
  Gateway Towers, Suite 235
  Pittsburgh, Pennsylvania
Owners: Mr. and Mrs. Eric Bohlin
Location: West Cornwall, Connecticut
Engineers: Rist-Frost Associates
Contractor: Olsen Brothers
Photographer: Joseph Molitor

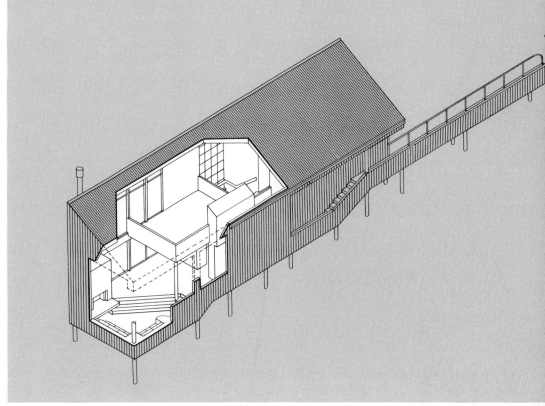

OPEN TO
L.R. BELOW

DEN

STOR.

BR.

UPPER LEVEL

L.R.

D.R.

KIT.

UTIL.

BR.

LOWER LEVEL

0   5   10 FT.

Seen from the entry side, the long shape is a transition from dark evergreen to sunlit forest (photo opposite, top). The view toward the kitchen (opposite, bottom) reveals the partial enclosure of the kitchen in a greenhouse-like structure. The stairs to the upper level (below, left) lead to the intimately scaled den (below, right) with its balcony-overlook of the living room.

The light gray finish of both walls and stained-oak flooring forms a soft-but-defined contrast to the darker colors of siding and structure.

10:

Actor Michael Tolan, an avid tennis player, commissioned architects Gwathmey-Siegel to design his house on this East Hampton site adjacent to a house and studio Charles Gwathmey designed for his parents six years ago. The set-back requirements, established by zoning ordinances, fixed the location of the tennis court and influenced the decision to use it as a design device and site reference. The other two elements in Tolan's program—a main house and guest quarters—were joined in a way that assures maximum privacy and provides a backstop wall for one end of the court. The roof of the low guest quarters has been developed as a deck overlooking the court to the north and the beach to the south. A long wall, its stability reinforced by steel pipe buttressing, encloses the court on the east and acts as a visual and acoustical screen.

The main house is zoned horizontally, with master bedroom on the lower level separated from guest bedrooms by the main entrance. Living room, dining room and kitchen, conceived as a single space, occupy the second level, and a small, triangular roof deck occurs over the kitchen and dining area. Storage is handled nicely in a variety of freestanding, sculptural dividers and cabinets.

Few other architects work with such skill in this particular design vocabulary. The softly-rounded, voluptuous forms are played off against the square-edged geometry with a sure hand, and where the visual lines of force are complex—as over the living-dining room (photo overleaf)—Gwathmey has resolved them in orderly spatial patterns. The details, as in Gwathmey's earlier houses, are dressy and carefully stated, and contribute importantly to a pervading atmosphere of elegance and ease.

Architects: Gwathmey-Siegel
    154 West 57th Street
    New York, New York
Owner: Michael Tolan
Location: Eastern Long Island,
    New York
Contractor: John Caramagna
Photographer: William Maris

SITE PLAN

10

N

The unexpected camera angle above is from the upper level deck and looks through a clerestory down into the living room and out to the horizon.

Photo below right is the master bedroom of the Tolan house with built-in dresser that also houses a television. Above right: the kitchen with built-in storage and a pass-through to the dining area.

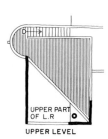

UPPER PART OF L.R

UPPER LEVEL

KIT.

D.R.

L.R.

MIDDLE LEVEL

PLAYRM.

BR. BR. BR.

BR.

LOWER LEVEL

Photos: Edith Reichman

11:

Twenty years ago the formality of this house, at Fire Island near New York City, would have seemed much less remarkable than it does today. At that time, the informality that characterizes so much of today's domestic architecture was the exception. But it was not architect Jim McLeod's intention either to buck the trend or to hark back to the past when he designed the building. Fire Island, interesting because it has no regular automobile traffic (residents walk on sidewalk-width boardwalks pulling red coaster wagons when they go to the store), is little more than a wide sand bar. Thus, all construction must be on pilings, usually locust posts driven to refusal into the sand. McLeod's scheme, two pavilions on a platform around a pool, is quite straightforward under the circumstances. The pool rests upon the grade and the wood-slat platform (above) has a minimal sub-structure. The pavilions, which use laminated wood beams to provide clear span interiors, also have very simple foundations since there are relatively few supports. But site conditions were not the only determinants of this spare and elegant house. The program called for "a 'super-neutral' background for the owners and selections of their art collection."

Architect: JAMES McLEOD. *Location:* Fire Island, New York. *Consultants:* Holly Neal (acoustics); Kilpatrick and Gellert (lighting). *Contractor:* Joseph Chasas.

Edith Reichman

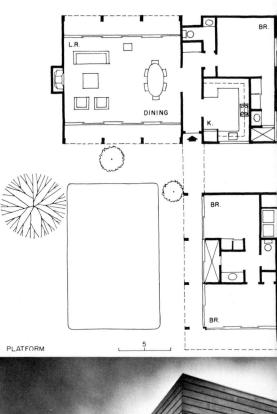

L.R.

DINING

K.

BR.

BR.

BR.

PLATFORM

5

Otto Baitz photos

All the major glazing, in painted aluminum sliding doors, is recessed four feet from the face of the cedar-sheathed columns. Restrained and carefully-studied wood detailing is the key to the building's elegance. The radii at juncture of column and fascia were formed by kerfed boards that were then filled and sanded. Cool understatement is the quality of the interiors as well (right). Furnishings chosen by the architect complement the design and draw attention to pieces from the owners' art collection. A corner bedroom (across page bottom) looks toward the pool and into the pine woods.

Maris/Semel photos

12:

Within the simplest of shapes—a 30- by 30- by 27-ft cube—Julian and Barbara Neski have created a house that offers constantly varying experiences of space, of indoor and outdoor living, and of view.

The architects explain the complexity within simplicity this way: "The house was designed as a weekend retreat for a young couple and their three children. The site is wooded, and on the edge of an inlet which opens to the bay and the ocean.

"It was decided to develop a design which would enable one to experience the trees, water, and sky from constantly shifting planes of reference and cross reference; in effect, to establish a continuous vertical movement through 11 levels [see plan], culminating in a final [and most dramatic of all] view of the sea from the roof deck."

The plan, a 30-foot-square angled on the site, is divided into four squares which coil up and down about the central stairwell spine. The exterior expresses the shifting levels of space with windows and porch openings of varied—but artfully proportioned—width and height. Further—and such "complexities" work well against the essentially simple mass of the house—the attached elements of entry bridge and stair cylinder contrast pleasantly and balance with elements that are incised into the smooth surface of the cube.

Architects: BARBARA and JULIAN NESKI—associate: Ronald Bechtol. *Owners:* Mr. and Mrs. Peter Simon. *Location:* Remsenburg, Long Island, New York. *Interior designers:* Neski Associates. *Structural engineer:* Stanley Gleit. *Contractor:* Vern & Ben Warner.

Entry bridge leads to one of the many spaces incised from the cube shape. This porch leads to the entry hall and kitchen, and from there the main circulation space moves in four-step jumps up to the living spaces, including a two-story high living room (photos next pages), and—still higher—a study, master bedroom, and roof deck. A second stair in the entry leads down to two more bedrooms and a bath. There are 11 levels in all. A circular stair tower short-circuits the roof deck-living room-lower deck levels.

The house is finished with 1 by 4 fir, with flush joints; sealed and bleached.

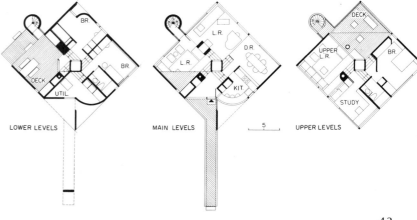

LOWER LEVELS   MAIN LEVELS   UPPER LEVELS

The interiors—with their constantly changing levels and unexpected openings to the outside and the various decks—offer constantly changing views and spatial experiences. Opposite page: the main living space with, at top, an opening to the roof deck and, at rear, a more intimate music and seating area. The kitchen (above), with its curved dining bar is on level with the dining room; it in turn opens to the music area (left). Below: two other views of the living room.

Inside finishes are drywall for walls and ceiling, oak strip flooring.

13:

This year-round vacation house reveals itself from the long approach road, first in end elevation, later in series of graduated glimpses rotating through 90 degrees to full front elevation. The site is a broad open meadow in Ashley Falls, Massachusetts—a site without tree cover, neighboring houses or other prominent foreground features. Because the site was remote from architects Julian and Barbara Neski's New York practice, and because they were unfamiliar with local building conditions, the Neski's developed a straightforward, rectilinear plan dimensioned to the standard window and sliding door module. This interior volume, in two levels, encloses all the main spaces of the house in a series of beautifully proportioned rooms that flow into each other logically and smoothly. The upper-level living room provides panoramic views of other meadows beyond the site and mountains in the distance. The kitchen, on the lower level, is outsized because the family includes three daughters who like to cook and spend a good deal of time preparing food.

Outside the glass core, the house wears a mask of wood shaped into covered decks and stairs that gives the whole design a rich, sculptural massing and lively visual interest. Textural interest is obtained by applying the wood siding in patterns both vertical and diagonal.

The interior finishes include oak strip and slate floors, drywall partitions and ceilings. Much of the furniture and cabinetry is built-in. Outside, the house is sheathed in cedar with bleaching oil applied to assure even weathering to a soft gray brown. All openings are double glazed, as the house gets substantial use on winter weekends and vacations.

Kitchen, family room, dining area and porch share the lower level. Above are the bedrooms and the more formal living room. A circular stair links the two levels.

Architects: Barbara and Julian Neski
18 East 53rd Street
New York, New York
Owners: Dr. and Mrs. Alan Frisch
Location: Ashley Falls, Massachusetts
Engineers: Robert Silman (structural)
Contractor: Joseph Maloney
Photographer: Norman McGrath

The living room upstairs sits squarely over the entrance and family room. Windows in the living room are protected by an overhang and located to provide panoramic views of this splendid site and surrounding.

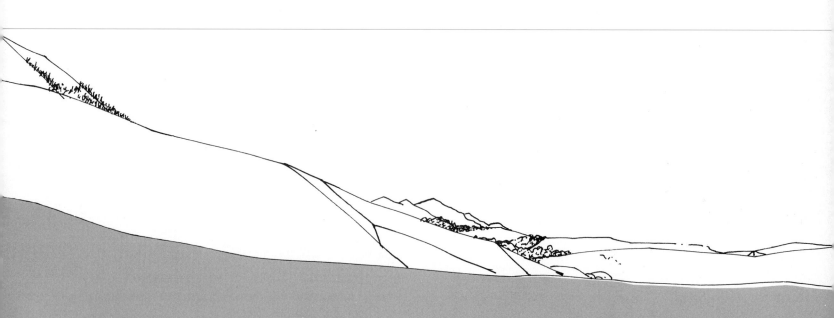

Ten ski and hillside houses

1:

Making use of an existing stone terrace and walls, architects Booth and Nagle have designed this large vacation house on a northern Minnesota lake to provide the best possible view for each room. Pivoting around a major room, 34 feet square and 18 feet high, which relates to all other interior spaces and the terrace, the design creates a series of indoor and outdoor spaces within a simple visual framework. It was detailed to facilitate construction by local workmen, including flat trusses which span the large space. Interior and exterior walls are sheathed in clear white cedar vertical siding. All openings toward the lake are large-scale, three panel units with bronze-tinted glass in the black aluminum frames. The interiors were also done by the architects who carefully chose the furniture to relate well to the cedar walls and the oak floors. All furniture in the main room (page 55) has natural leather upholstery.

Architects: LAURENCE BOOTH and JAMES NAGLE of Booth and Nagle. *Location:* Northern Minnesota. *Engineers:* Weisenger-Holland Ltd. (structural); Wallace and Migdal, Inc. (mechanical and electrical). *Interior design:* Booth and Nagle. *Contractor:* Arnold Seastedt.

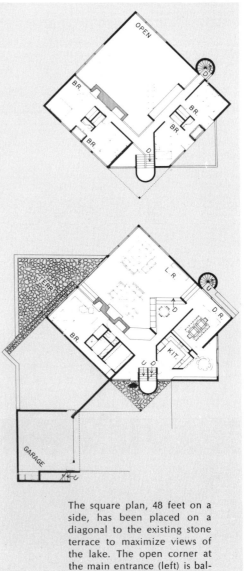

The square plan, 48 feet on a side, has been placed on a diagonal to the existing stone terrace to maximize views of the lake. The open corner at the main entrance (left) is balanced by a projecting breakfast room.

Phil Turner photos

2: The open and attractive sites usually chosen for vacation houses are often a major influence on architectural form. Thus this house in the White Mountains, used for skiing weekends and vacations, makes good use of a sloping, wooded site and expresses an appropriate sense of shelter from winter winds.

Patz/Lisanti, Inc. photos

The logical combination of masonry
and frame construction gives a
crisp clarity to the house (below)
and the sheltering roof appears
to float above the band of south-
facing windows. The massive
chimney not only stabilizes the
structure but provides a suitably-
scaled fireplace. From the
built-in couch, skiers can watch
the sun set on distant peaks.

The wooded slope facing south toward the Presidential range of the White Mountains is perfect for a winter vacation house. Architects Huygens and Tappé have not failed to make good use of it. A masonry shell of striated concrete block—especially visible across page—protects the two-story frame structure inside it from heavy north winds at the same time that it forms an extremely sheltered entry. On the sunny south side, glass walls and a balcony reach out to the splendid view. Although the massing is entirely symmetrical, including two narrow stairways from entry to balcony, interior planning is entirely free. Three bedrooms, some with four bunks each, along with a recreation area, have been fitted into the lower floor. The narrow hemlock clapboards used on the balcony also are used on the interior walls and ceilings. The interiors and most of the furniture were designed by the architects.

WINTER VACATION HOUSE, White Mountains, New Hampshire. Architects: *Huygens and Tappé*. Engineers: *Souza and True* (structural); *William R. Ginns* (mechanical); *Lotters and Mason Assocs.* (electrical). Contractor: *Philip Robertson*.

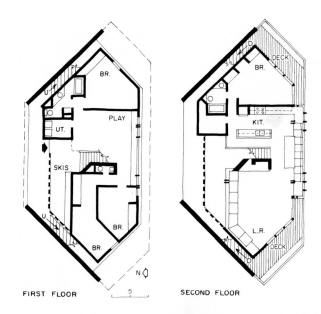

FIRST FLOOR   SECOND FLOOR

3:

Sited in a birch grove in Colorado's high country, its eaves drifted and its fireplace ablaze,
the Hodgson house is the stuff of which skiers' fantasies are made. More important,
it is an architectural opportunity that Eliot Noyes has realized with a special distinction.

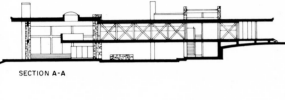

SECTION A-A

UPPER LEVEL

LOWER LEVEL

The logic of the plan derives from the sloping site and from the program requirement for individual and small-group privacy. The living and sleeping quarters are treated as separate architectural elements linked by an enclosed bridge at the upper level. The main entry, beneath the bridge, is on level with the kitchen and dining areas. The living room, five steps above, is treated as a raised platform that leads by an open stair to an intimate, balcony lounge and the bridge. Framed by a pair of timber trusses, and partially sheathed in cedar, the bridge connects to a two-story block of bedrooms.

The house is framed in laminated wood beams and tendoned with steel at the connections to the bridge. Finish materials are rough-sawn cedar or stone veneer at outside walls, cedar for ceilings and soffits, brick pavers for dining and living room floors. Detailing is elegant throughout.

Spectacular views to the north and west are framed by unusually large openings that act as foils for the heavy masonry walls. The general openness of plan and the use of partial levels contribute to a feeling of spatial liveliness—a feeling reinforced by flexible lighting and a generous scale.

View from the living room showing the dining area below and the connection to the bridge above. The door, at rear, leads to the maid's quarters. Bedroom has generous openings but maintains a strong sense of shelter.

HODGSON HOUSE, Snowmass, Colorado. Architects: *Eliot Noyes & Associates*. Engineers: *Viggo Bonnesen & Associates* (structural); *John Altieri* (mechanical). Lighting consultants: *Sylvan Schemitz & Associates*. Interiors: *Sewell and Charity*. Contractor: *H. E. Anderson, Inc.*

Resawn cedar plywood and prefabricated greenhouse sections are the key visual elements in this combination house and studio nestled into the Santa Cruz Mountains of California. The owners are two artists and teachers who preferred to live casually in a house that gave them a sense of openness and light. They also wanted to garden, maintain a small orchard, and keep horses; and they didn't want to have to worry about using their house as a base for these kinds of activities. A greenhouse for gardening during the colder months suggested itself as a natural connector between the house and the studio, where the owners work and hold small classes. Then, greenhouse sections suggested themselves as an equally natural way to provide openness and light throughout. They are stacked and staggered to admit light into both floors of the house (left), or used singly to light the entrance hall or to cover a projecting balcony (right).

4: This house is a robust manifestation of a very particular way of living. Architects around San Francisco seem traditionally to have been less willing than most to bend with the prevailing stylistic winds, though from time to time they have sent some special ones of their own blowing East. If the architect of this house caught his way of designing from older and more famous teachers, then he and his clients have managed to transmute the lessons into something that is unique and altogether their own.

The stock greenhouse sections seem pleasantly domestic, even though it is possible to see in them recollections of the finely honed work of James Stirling. The interior spaces, too, must owe something to cousins at the Sea Ranch, and the rough plywood finish is an easygoing industrial counterpart to the kinds of materials Bay Region architects have favored for years. Yet the house manages to be powerfully different. It is individualistic, even good-naturedly homely, and it is brimming over with the sense that it is just the kind of house its owners wanted, and knew they could not get prepackaged.

It was they, in fact, who ordered the plywood finish. It was also they who found themselves, as the designs were being worked out, in the familiar *cul-de-sac* of wanting more than they could afford, and not being willing to build in stages. So they rolled up their sleeves and built the house themselves, with assistance from the architect and only one full-time carpenter.

Only time and the owners will tell whether or not all the decisions were good ones—whether, for instance, so much uncontrolled sunlight inside will really seem desirable, or whether the sense of openness created by the plywood walls sliding from inside past the glass to the outside won't be diminished as the plywood outside weathers and, on the inside, doesn't.

In any case, the house is a cheering expression of the owners' special taste, and of their architect's ability to nourish it. Though the latter member of this triumvirate freely borrowed from his colleagues, he let the house not only be different, but also quietly and blessedly unrhetorical; this is a quality to be greatly treasured.

Architect: PETER BEHN of Behn and Gavin. *Owners:* Mr. and Mrs. Robert Lozano. *Location:* Santa Cruz County, California.

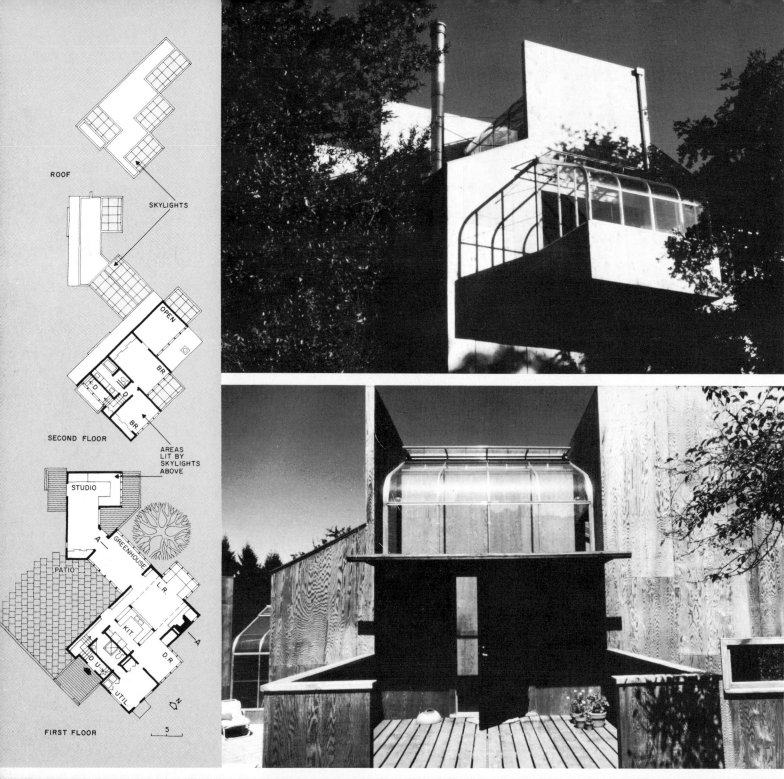

ROOF

SKYLIGHTS

SECOND FLOOR

OPEN

BR

BR

AREAS
LIT BY
SKYLIGHTS
ABOVE

STUDIO

GREENHOUSE

PATIO

L.R.

KIT

D.R.

UTIL

FIRST FLOOR

5

N

Inside the house, cedar plywood remains the finish material, and there is an abundance of natural light in all of the rooms. A bedroom and a bath on the second floor are shown on the right above; adjacent on the right is the greenhouse, seen through sliding barn doors. Above and on the left is the living room, lit by two greenhouse sections, and penetrated from the second floor of the house by a small balcony.

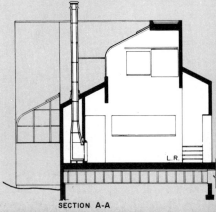

SECTION A-A

Jeremiah O. Bragstad photos

SUNDECK

LOFT

DRESS

TUB

SAUNA

INGLENOOK

KIT

DINING

MAIN FLOOR

DECK

5: An indigenous material and a modest form have been combined to produce an intriguing yet uncomplicated vacation house. Architects McCue Boone Tomsick make the most of a downhill approach (above) by sheathing the roof as well as the walls with tongue-and-groove redwood boards. The unifying effect of the common material makes the house seem smaller and more simple than it proves to be upon entry (acrosspage). Yet such modesty is entirely appropriate when the site is an isolated and heavily forested hillside in the Santa Cruz Moutains of California, looking out over a valley preserve toward the Pacific Ocean. The angled wall, which follows the hip of the roof at the entry, provides protected entrance where those who

have walked down the hill from the parking area may remove muddy boots and winter coats before entering. That part of the house is oriented away from the winds but catches mid-day sun. End-grain redwood paving blocks form a parquet terrace that continues indoors as an important finish.

A very generous stairway within the single, large interior space makes vertical circulation an important generator of the functional relationships. Directly ahead, as one enters, a short flight of steps just past the kitchen leads to the level with four small rooms containing toilet facilities (including a sauna). To the right and up the stairs is the bedroom. Again to the right, and now outdoors, this squared spiral leads up to the sun-

deck in the treetops. Redwood boards also sheathe the interior completely; the ceiling boards are spaced slightly apart to assist in ventilation of the roof structure. Although the large space is beautifully detailed, it is clear that it was designed for unpretentious and relaxed vacation use. Within the large space, the eating area is adjacent to the strip kitchen. Under the ceiling formed by the bedroom floor, is an inglenook sitting area around a fireplace whose seating doubles as extra sleeping accommodation.

VACATION HOUSE, San Mateo County, California. Architects: *McCue Boone Tomsick*. Engineers: *Hirsh and Gray* (structural); *Marion, Cerbatos and Tomasi* (mechanical/electrical), General contractor. *Henry Knutzen Sons, Inc.*

A high degree of spatial integration is achieved within the house by the use of a single material—redwood—on walls, ceilings and floors. The square spiral stairway and the loft bedroom which opens onto the large space below also contribute to the unified feeling. Butted glazing in both downhill corner windows of the main floor room provide splendid diagonal views into the thick foliage while the slit windows illuminate the page for anyone reading on the built-in couch.

Morley Baer photos

6:

A south slope, densely wooded with Monterey Pines and overlooking Carmel Bay, is the site for this handsome pole house designed for sale by architects Smith & Larson. The decision to use pole supports simplified the foundation conditions, left the site as undisturbed as possible and, in general, minimized the difficulties and expense conventionally associated with building on a hillside.

Living spaces are arranged on three levels. Kitchen, dining, living room and master bedroom share the lowest level. Carport, study, guest room and bath occupy the middle level. The upper level is reserved for children's lofts and storage. Entrance and lofts face the street while the living areas open toward the south and the view.

The poles form an exterior framing system standing just outside the plane of the walls except that the lower level living spaces pivot around a single freestanding pole that supports a corner of the study above (photo page 74).

The house was built as a speculative venture by architects who wanted to expand their experience as they established their practice. In the absence of an owner with a precise program, the house might have become too personal—too fervid an expression of the designers' own attitudes and interests. Happily, that did not happen. While the conception is anything but timid, the apportionment of spaces is clearly functional and the designers have carefully avoided geometric extremes or oddly shaped volumes.

As a result, the house found an enthusiastic buyer almost at once. Lawrence Spector speaks lyrically of his new house: "I wanted to own it after we opened the front door . . . light, space, view in every direction . . . rain water running down the sheets of roof glass. We were under a waterfall. I could have indoor plants, a natural kind of decoration everywhere.

"I walked around the property in the next days, in the light of day, in the rain, at midnight. The house simply radiates from any position on the land. . . ."

This praise is not undeserved. The Spector house is beautifully tailored to its site and apparently just as well suited to the needs of its new owner.

Architects and engineers: SMITH & LARSON. *Owner:* Lawrence Albert Spector. *Location:* Pebble Beach, California. *General Contractor:* Smith & Larson.

The main entrance (photo left) is reached by means of a stair and bridge at the side of the house. The bridge is protected from the weather by the projection of the level above. A simply detailed deck (photo right) extends beyond the living room and provides an intimate space for outdoor dining.

Sunlight is brought deep into the interior of the living-dining space by glass panels cut into the pitched roof (photos right and above left). The second floor study draws sunlight from the same source. Thanks to careful design, the quality of natural light is exceptionally pleasant throughout the house.

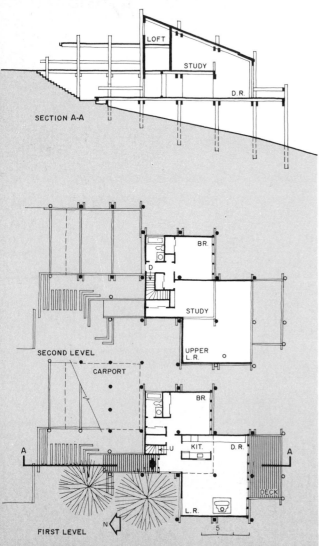

SECTION A-A

LOFT

STUDY

D.R.

SECOND LEVEL

CARPORT

BR.

D

STUDY

UPPER L.R.

BR.

KIT.

D.R.

DECK

L.R.

FIRST LEVEL

N

5

7:

A thousand feet above Aspen, on a southern slope of the Elk Range, architect Robin Molny has sited this angular, 3800-square-foot house for a couple whose shared love of the outdoors led them to this spectacular mountainside. Here, amid scrub oak and drifted snow, the battered walls of the Schumann house seem to grow out of the slope in a complex geometry of stepped, flat-roofed forms. The spatial cadences of the house are rather free and the elevations that result are lively and irregular.

The view from the living room is incomparable. Molny framed this panorama in a 40-foot-wide opening, then glazed the opening dramatically with four spectacular 10- by 10-foot panes of edge-glued ⅜-inch tempered plate glass (see photos, pp. 78 and 79).

Other interior spaces, turned 45 degrees off the living room axis, open more modestly but provide compelling views of Aspen on the valley floor below. Clerestories and hipped-roof skylights introduce daylight at unexpected but welcome intervals inside—as at the back wall of the living room or over the corner of the master bedroom.

The whole composition—down to the smallest triangular table—has the kind of character that suggests that design proceeded along intuitive tracks, daring much and fearing little. The results, if geometrically complex, have more than the excitement of novelty alone. The Schumann house is a vigorous, personal statement. Its planning and design are forceful responses to an extraordinary site. Its details, inside and out are particularized, and the manner of its furnishing reflects the owner's interests, tastes and lifestyle.

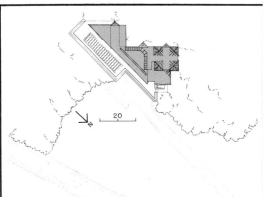

Stucco, over metal channels and lath, is the principal exterior finish. Inside, the owner—who is a painter—required and got large wall display areas of white plaster.

SECTION A-A

POOL · GAR. · L.R. · BR. · STUDIO

MAIN FLOOR

MECH. · BR. · L.R. · STUDIO · POOL · KIT. · A · A

UPPER FLOOR · BR. · BR.

Architect: Robin Molny
　　Box 96
　　Aspen, Colorado
Owner: W. Ford Schumann
Location: Aspen, Colorado
Engineer: KKBNA (structural)
Contractor: H.E. Anderson, Inc.
Photographer: Marc Neuhof

8:

A small turn-of-the-century carriage house has been transformed by architects Crissman & Solomon into a study and laboratory for its owner—and can serve as a self-sufficient guest house. Within the small building the architects have created an environment of great distinction and warmth.

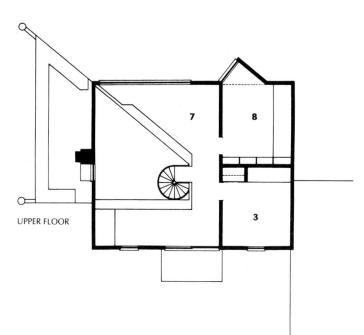

UPPER FLOOR

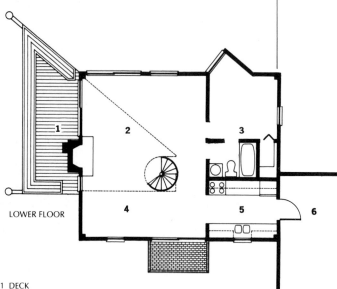

LOWER FLOOR

1 DECK
2 LIVING
3 BEDROOM
4 DINING
5 KITCHEN
6 BARN
7 READING GALLERY
8 STUDY

This renovated 60-year-old carriage house has been opened up to the west to afford its owners one of the most spectacular views in the greater Boston area. A very small building, only 25 by 30 feet, its lowest level is used as a garage and mechanical space. The main floor, which is at the same level as the barn floor with which it connects, has been transformed into a comfortable guest house with a living-dining area, a bedroom and a kitchen.

The second floor has become a mezzanine through the subtraction of a wedge-shaped portion. This judicious paring away adds to the volumetric complexity of the living-dining area, affording views upward to the roof and from the mezzanine downward to the main floor.

This solution was made practical by the existence of a solid wood beam, approximately 8 by 10 inches, which bisects the structure in the east-west direction and supports the second floor. It serves as the anchor for one end of the steel rod that became the necessary means of tying the south wall to the rest of the structure after the wedge-shaped portion of the floor had been removed. A vertical tie rod from which this beam is hung is part of the old structure and is connected to the trusses of the gambrel roof. Both the horizontal and vertical rods can be seen in the photographs opposite. The location of this beam determined the placement of the circular stair which ties into it at the second floor landing.

The old wood flooring which was removed was used for patching in the renovated areas. All the finished wood floors are made up of the old planks.

As the plans indicate, the south and west elevations were opened up as much as possible with the two-story living space and deck facing the view, and the smaller spaces arranged along the barn side of the building. The major view is captured from the study and the first floor bedroom by means of the angled windows which project from the west facade. The entire building was reclad in cedar shingles, except for the roof, which had been asphalt-shingled before the restoration. The cost without furniture was $20 per square foot.

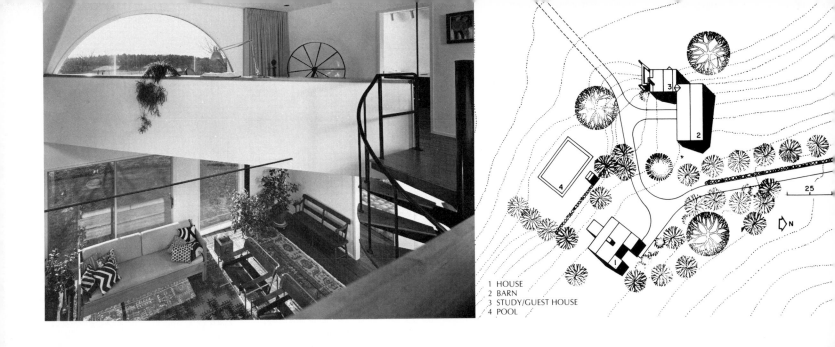

1 HOUSE
2 BARN
3 STUDY/GUEST HOUSE
4 POOL

The railing of the newly formed mezzanine is a continuous bookcase, which transforms the adjacent space into a reading gallery. The top of this bookcase serves as a useful ledge for plants and books and also provides reference space. Opening off the reading gallery is the owner's study with custom-built bookcases, files and a work ledge neatly fitted into the gambrel roof. From this study window the owner enjoys a magnificent view of the entire Boston skyline.

KIMBALL CARRIAGE HOUSE, Andover, Massachusetts. Owner: *Mr. and Mrs. John W. Kimball.* Architects: *Crissman & Solomon.* Structural engineer: *Eugene Hamilton.* Contractor: *Fitzgerald Henderson Porter Inc.*

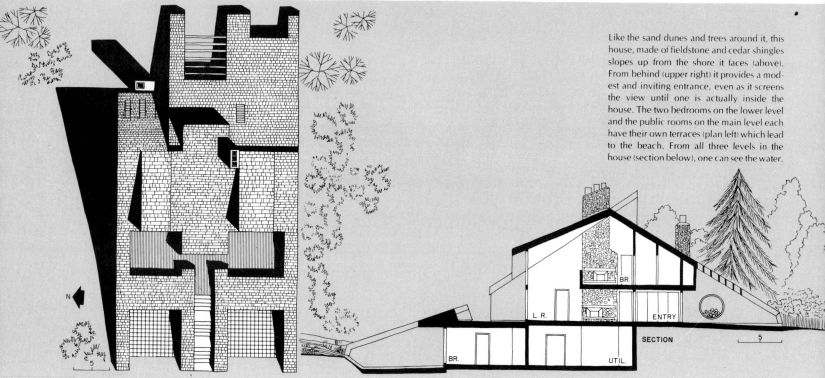

Like the sand dunes and trees around it, this house, made of fieldstone and cedar shingles slopes up from the shore it faces (above). From behind (upper right) it provides a modest and inviting entrance, even as it screens the view until one is actually inside the house. The two bedrooms on the lower level and the public rooms on the main level each have their own terraces (plan left) which lead to the beach. From all three levels in the house (section below), one can see the water.

Balthazar Korab photos

9: This year-round vacation house is notable for the way it merges into its site while still remaining a strong shape, and for its interior arrangement, which provides a generous complex of communal and private spaces for the owners, their guests, and their six children.

The site, which faces westward over Lake Michigan, was a small sand bowl surrounded by thickets of pine, spruce and birch trees. The house was designed to fill in the bowl and echo the profile of the landscape which sweeps up from the water's edge to the tall trees behind. While doing this, though, it also manages to evoke a host of disparate images: from the back it looks something like an old-fashioned shingled house sunk deep into the ground, and from the front

like a set of precarious ski jumps, or even, with a little imagination, like the Great Sphinx at Giza.

For all these peculiar riches, the house shows an admirable attempt to be polite to its surroundings, without being so polite that it loses its own identity.

Inside, the children's bedrooms are dormitories placed on a separate floor, with their own access to the beach. Above them are the more public rooms—two living areas (again with access to the beach), a dining area and a kitchen, which is placed so that it can conveniently supply meals taken either indoors or outdoors, on the terrace or on the beach.

The master bedroom and guest room are both on open balconies above the main floor, though each

has its own private bath and dressing room, and the former has an uncommon luxury, a fireplace.

Because of its careful provisions for privacy in some parts, because of the placement of the kitchen which allows it to be used from a number of different directions, and because of the more open arrangement of the public spaces, the house gives its occupants many opportunities to savor the pleasures of the site and of each other's company, while also allowing them to retreat to their own special quarters.

Architects: WILLIAM KESSLER AND ASSOCIATES, *Owners:* Mr. and Mrs. Walter Briggs, III. *Location:* L'arbre Croche, Harbor Springs, Michigan. *Contractor:* Walter H. Desimpel, Co.

UPPER FLOOR

MAIN FLOOR

LOWER FLOOR

5

The living area on the left is designed primarily for children, and, since it is open to the kitchen (below right) it is also especially useful for dining. The living area on the right is more obviously separated from the kitchen and becomes, when necessary, a place for adults to gather, away from cooking activities and away from the children. Both living areas open onto a deck above the bedrooms on the lower floor and, from that, onto the beach.

10:

Merg Ross photos

This house is one of the most recent
successful examples of housing at The Sea Ranch.
It is unpretentious, fitting into its site
and capitalizing on the site's amenities
to create an environment that is warm and natural,
filled with light and open to splendid views.

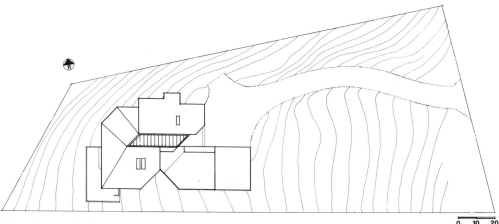

0 10 20

The site is a highly visible, open hillside with magnificent views of the Pacific Ocean and the rugged northern California coast. The house is set on the lower portion of the property to obtain as sweeping a panorama as possible, since trees and large bushes to the north would have obscured part of the view had the house been situated on the upper portion. A row of pines to south and west filters the view in that direction and screens the house. In response to the nature of the place and to minimize intrusion of the house on the site, the profile of the structure is kept low, and the pitch of the roofs visually ties the house to the land. To continue the character set by the first buildings at The Sea Ranch, the house has an almost stark look, to which details—no overhangs, no moldings on any of the openings—as well as the plain board siding contribute. Although deck space is provided on the sunny sides, west and south, the most usable outdoor space is a partially protected courtyard on the east between the studio and garage. The angled courtyard fence, at the southeast corner of the studio, breaks the line of the house on the south side. There was little disturbance of indigenous grasses and plants and the owners have retained the natural landscaping. The use of redwood siding and cedar shingles, left to weather, help to relate the house to its natural surroundings.

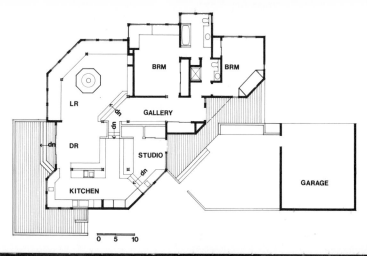

The open plan, variations in ceiling heights, and a change in levels create a feeling of spaciousness in the main living areas. The entrance gallery, bedrooms and a studio for Mrs. Barrell are located on the upper level; and the living room, dining room and kitchen are on a level a few feet lower. The owners wanted "no dark places" in the interiors, so skylights were placed where light was needed most. The largest skylight, running the length of the entrance gallery, allows abundant light to fill the entry hall and provide the "warm welcome" the owners asked for, to flow into the interior of the living room, and to light the walkway between the studio and dining room. The length of the hall affords display space for the owners' rugs and for books. The main living areas are oriented to views on the north, west and south through a band of windows which bring the view "into scale with the individual," a particular request of the owners. Rough sawn red cedar walls and fir ceilings give warmth to the interiors and help relate them to the outside surroundings. Bronze-tinted glass in the main living areas cuts glare.

RESIDENCE FOR MR. & MRS. RICHARD BARRELL, The Sea Ranch, California. Architect: *Donald Jacobs.* Structural engineer: *Fook Z. Lee.* General contractor: *Mathew D. Sylvia.*

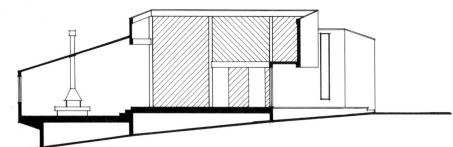

The studio (above) on the upper level separates the work area from the dining room and has a view to the west. There are two skylights, side by side, in this area—one bringing overhead light onto the studio desk, the other allowing light to enter the walkway between dining room and studio. The guest room is small but appears larger because of a high ceiling, two floor-to-ceiling windows and three bunk beds tiered in a built-in frame (right). The kitchen (top) is longer than usual and provides ample counter space to allow both the owners to use it simultaneously.

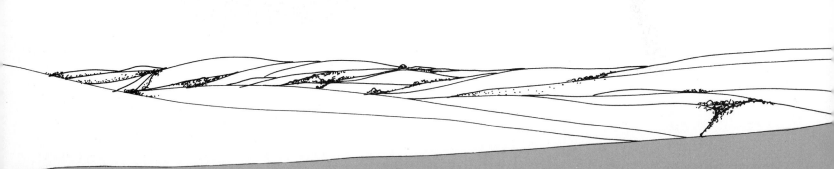

Nineteen weekend

and summer houses

1:

The majestic site and the minimal support conditions it afforded were prime determinants in the design of this Colorado mountain cabin. Four 16-inch diameter caissons, each anchored eight feet into bedrock, support a central wedge form that houses the main living area. Steel braces from these caissons pick up the roof loads and floor cantilevers of the two satellite wedge forms. This family of interlocking elements creates a lively and intricate geometry—a theme playfully developed by triangular window openings—but the use of a single exterior finish material—1- by 6-inch redwood siding on walls and roofs—gives the massing a welcome homogeneity. Adding to this unity is a constant roof slope of 3 on 2, which ends up in a volume of strongly vertical spatial development.

The cabin is structured of 2- by 6-inch studs sheathed on both sides with ½-inch plywood glued and nailed to form a stressed skin panel. The plywood, taped and painted white, is the primary interior finish material.

The exterior walls are sandwiched with six-inch batts of glass fiber, which give sufficient insulation to heat the entire cabin with electric baseboard heaters of 58,000 Btu/hr capacity.

The owners asked that the cabin disturb the natural beauty of the site as little as possible. They got their wish—and a great deal more.

Architects: Arley Rinehart Associates
  2345 Seventh Street
  Denver, Colorado
Clients: Mr. and Mrs. Ben Collins
*Present owners: Dr. and Mrs.
  Nelson E. Mohler*
Location: Perry Park, Colorado
Engineers:
  Ron Frickel (structural)
  J. J. Blank (mechanical)
  R. W. Thompson (foundation)
Contractor: Ben Collins
Photographers: Richard Springgate,
  Robert McConnell

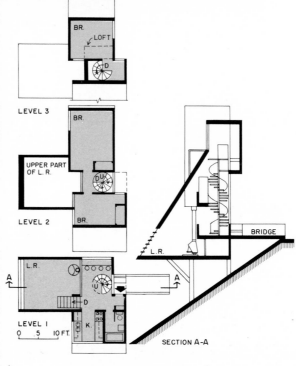

LEVEL 3
LOFT
BR.
D

UPPER PART OF L.R.
BR.
DW

LEVEL 2
BR.

LEVEL 1
L.R.
U
D
K.
0 5 10 FT.

BRIDGE
L.R.
SECTION A-A

2: At first glance, the plan of the Stephen Kaplan house in Easthampton, New York may seem no more than a modish exercise in diagonal geometry. Two characteristics of the site, however, make it work very well indeed. First, it is set in a landscape nursery whose shrubs and trees have a strong linear pattern. The vertical lines on the plan (opposite) relate to that geometry. Second, the major diagonals, especially in the family-living room wing, are parallel to the prevailing breezes. In August, when everyone else has closed up the windows and switched on the air conditioner, this house is full of gently moving air. Barbara and Julian Neski have played with that openness in visual terms as well. The angular, rather massive facade that visitors approach from the south literally dissolves into a space (page 102) so filled with light that it hardly seems enclosed at all. The substantial exterior forms of bleached cedar siding contrast with a white interior that has two enormous triangular skylights. One of them can be seen (above) casting afternoon shadows high on the living room wall.

Architects: BARBARA AND JULIAN NESKI. *Owners:* Mr. and Mrs. Stephen Kaplan. *Location:* Easthampton, New York. *Engineers:* Stanley Gleit (structural); Weber & Grahn (mechanical). *Contractor:* Peter Wazlo.

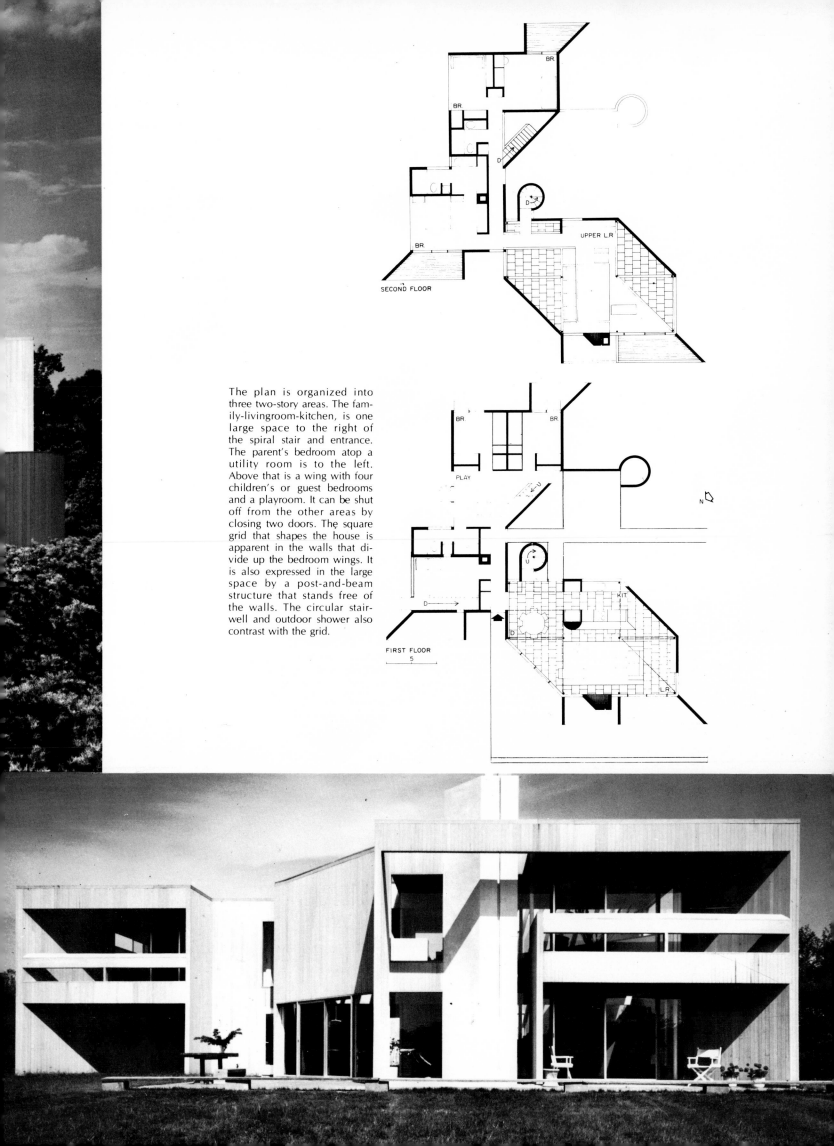

SECOND FLOOR

The plan is organized into three two-story areas. The family-livingroom-kitchen, is one large space to the right of the spiral stair and entrance. The parent's bedroom atop a utility room is to the left. Above that is a wing with four children's or guest bedrooms and a playroom. It can be shut off from the other areas by closing two doors. The square grid that shapes the house is apparent in the walls that divide up the bedroom wings. It is also expressed in the large space by a post-and-beam structure that stands free of the walls. The circular stairwell and outdoor shower also contrast with the grid.

BR

BR

BR

UPPER L.R

BR

BR

PLAY

N

KIT

D

FIRST FLOOR
5

L R

"The family-living room wing is meant to be an active, dynamic light-filled space; the system of columns, beams, skylights, open wells and glass combine to provide a setting for family activity and entertaining on two levels," say the Neskis. Four views from differing heights and positions within the space testify to the excitement of the room. The upper area is meant to be used for quieter entertaining in conjunction with the parents' suite.

William Maris

The stairway in the children's wing (left), with open risers and a solid baluster, is a playful switch on usual practice. The white door at the head of the stairs and the one beneath separate the children completely from the rest of the house when that is desired. The parents' bedroom (above) has its own large balcony. It is near the children yet connects, by a bridge, directly to the upper level sitting area in the family-living room wing and to the first floor by the circular stair.

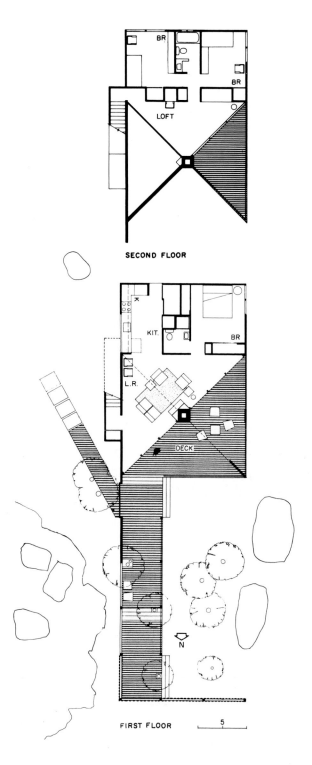

SECOND FLOOR

FIRST FLOOR

5

3: This year-round vacation home by architects Mayers & Schiff is located in the Pocono Mountains of Pennsylvania. The site is long and narrow with one end fronting on a pond. Part of the site— a small rocky ledge and a half dozen very large boulders strewn about—was high-

ly picturesque but unsuitable for building on. The primary aim of the architects in siting the house was to incorporate this space into the design of the house itself. Approaching the house the first view is of a continuous sloping redwood wall which slices across the narrow dimension

of the site and is punctured by a glossy white barn door. The wall hides all views of a pond and the large boulders, until the barn door is slid open—whereupon one is, quite unexpectedly, back outside! But not quite, for while part of the long wall forms one wall of the house, the

William Maris photos

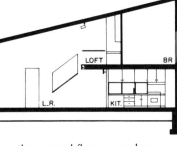

The supergraphics of the Benenson house, designed by artist Florence Cassen, are an extension of the architects' basic diagonal concept. A continuous green stripe has been painted across the longest single wall surface (stairwell, below) in the house. A combination of sliding panels between the living room and other ground floor spaces have also been painted with bands of varying widths. As panels are re-arranged in various ways, the stripes regroup to form new designs.

remainder is backed by a two-level open deck covered by a trellis. Both deck and trellis serve as wind bracing for this section of the wall. From the entry side one cannot tell where the house (the interior living spaces) ends and the long deck (one of the outdoor living spaces) behind the wall begins; a fact that also intensifies the tie between the architecture and the natural spatial qualities of the site. At the point where the view of boulders on both sides, the cliff, and the whole natural setting is at its best, the wall is cut away, allowing nature to frame another type of more open outdoor space. This area is the favorite outdoor sitting area for the residents. The unusual family makeup dictated special indoor space requirements: with four children varying from young ones still at home to older married ones who visit frequently, the Benensons find themselves with an overflow crowd on some weekends and completely alone on others. Rather than build a large house with many bedrooms which would be "dead" space much of the time, the architects decided to limit the fixed bedrooms and provide a large sleeping

A variety of indoor and out-door spaces—and some that are not exactly either—provide the occupants of this Pennsylvania second home by architects Mayers & Schiff with living areas for every mood and weather change. The house has been carefully sited and designed not simply to sit in nor merely blend with its pleasant natural setting, but rather the most interesting features of the terrain have been integrated into the design of the house itself. This is achieved for the most part by the multi-level deck that extends the house into the woods, and by the partially roofed-over deck that brings the outdoors into the main structural volume. The design of the house is all the more impressive in view of the fact that little site work was necessary for the architect's goal to be accomplished. The house cost about $33,000.

loft with built-in bunk beds for guests. The sleeping loft, with its built-in work desk and adjacent outdoor deck, serves as a study for the Benensons during the less-populated weekends. The main form of the house is based on a square cut into overlapping triangles on various levels—a kind of tri-level tic-tac-toe—with a fireplace and chimney at the square's center. The long sliding glass wall of the triangular living room is oriented towards a view of the boulders and pond. The living room is two stories high in the space formed by the overlapping triangular loft.

Architects: ROBERT A. MAYERS and JOHN C. SCHIFF
of Mayers & Schiff
Penthouse 45 East 51st Street, New York, New York
Owners: Dr. and Mrs. A. S. Benenson
Location: Hawley, Pennsylvania
Structural Engineer: Henry Gorlin
Mechanical Engineer: Seymour Berkowitz
Landscape Architects: Mayers & Schiff
Graphics: Florence Cassen
Contractor: Kreck-Myer

Milton Weinstock photos

Wooden panels roll across the large glazed areas on the first floor (photos at top on facing page) when the owners are away; and stack neatly, below.

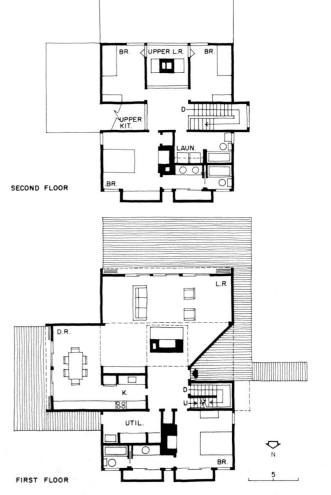

SECOND FLOOR

FIRST FLOOR

4: The austere, four-square self-sufficiency of the traditional American farmhouse is evoked by the exterior of this vacation house in Dublin, New Hampshire. Yet the interior, organized around the same central hall as the farmhouse, is rich in openness, informality and spatial variety.

In many ways, the problems facing those who build in northern New Hampshire have not changed in two hundred years. Therefore, the resemblance to old wood buildings is not surprising. Narrow cedar clapboards, parallel to the roof, and generous cornerboards, clearly traditional, are here used to emphasize the sweep of the two low wings away from the solid two-story main block. The diagonals at once tie the building to the land and thrust the matching half-gables to the sky.

This articulation of the gable, not to be found in old farm houses to be sure, permits a clerestory above the second floor hall. This unexpected, almost invisible light source fills the top of the house, the stairway, the kitchen and the two-story space around the chimney with light on the dreariest day.

The living room, right, conveys the clarity of the internal organization. A substantial wood and steel truss, spanning 26 feet, supports the structure and allows the chimney of the ironspot brick fireplace to stand free in the eight-foot square space. Thus in even such an intensely planned house, one can share from the upper hall, or the children's bedrooms, the activities on the lower floor.

BURNHAM HOUSE, Dublin, New Hampshire. Owners: *Mr. and Mrs. Daniel Burnham.* Architects: *Willis N. Mills, Jr. and Timothy Martin.* Engineers: *Paul Pantano* (structural); *Sanford O. Hess* (mechanical). Contractor: *Bergeron Construction Co.*

5:

Without power tools, without heavy equipment, without, in fact, outside help of any important kind, the Kindorf family, five-strong, built this appealing, three-level cabin on a two-acre site in Plumas County, California. The site is choked with pine and dips down to a large creek where swimming and trout fishing are seasonal preoccupations. The cabin was built over a period of three summers with cabinetwork and furniture construction occupying the long winter months in between.

The cabin has no electricity. Light is provided by kerosene lamps and heat by a Franklin stove. A 500-gallon, gravity-fed water tank supplies domestic needs and sewage wastes are chemically treated and stored. The absence of modern conveniences is in no way deprivative, for the family agrees that the simplified life style that results is fun and greatly heightens the sense of place.

Clad in cedar board and batten over plywood sheathing and 4- by 4-inch wood studs, the cabin has a simplicity and structural logic plainly visible in the photos. Its living and sleeping arrangements have a pleasant informality and its detailing and finishes are minimal.

Because of its inherent modesty and the very special circumstances surrounding its construction, the Kindorf cabin was built for the astonishingly low figure of $5 per square foot.

Architect and owner: Robert Kindorf
    245 Draeger Drive
    Moraga, California
Location: Plumas County, California
Contractors: The Kindorf family
Photographer: Philip Molten

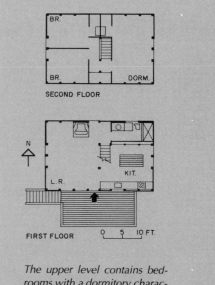

SECOND FLOOR

FIRST FLOOR

N

L.R.   KIT.

0   5   10 FT.

The upper level contains bedrooms with a dormitory character. The middle level, reached from the bedrooms by a stairladder, includes living, dining, kitchen and bath. The lowest level (not shown in plan) is an equipment storage area with an earthen floor.

To ease the erection process, Kindorf framed out the floors in doubled 2x6s, bolted in place, and the roof in 2x8s, also paired. Floor planking is white fir, roof is galvanized sheet.

6:

Woven into a spruce grove on the Maine coast, this beautifully restrained vacation house was built for a man who is an author/scholar, interested in public service. Among his wife's varied interests are calligraphy and cooking. Their children are grown and living away but often visit, bringing family or friends when they do. The program, therefore, suggested flexibility. The site suggested modesty.

Barnes began by developing four separate structures: a studio tower with laundry below; a one-bedroom house with living, dining and kitchen; a two-story guest house and a high-ceilinged library/study. Each of the elements is shaped in simple, vernacular forms finished in wood shingle, each is artfully placed in relation to the others, and all are spun together by a rambling wood deck that opens at intervals to arresting coastal views. The whole composition keeps a respectful distance from the shoreline.

The detailing throughout the house is spare and elegant in its simplicity. The roof planes turn down into the wall planes, for instance, without the interruption of barge board or fascia. Trim around openings is so reticent it all but disappears. At one corner of the deck, however, just off the kitchen, the need for a shaded outdoor eating area produced a novel and pleasantly flamboyant series of details. The architect set a spinnaker on booms—a sail that can be adjusted to a range of sun angles by hand-operated winches mounted on the deck.

Though elegant in its details, the house has some of the same hardy character and stern New England virtues that we associate with the Maine fishing villages its massing seems to reflect. No roofs connect its four units and the access road stops two hundred feet short of the house.

Architect: Edward Larrabee Barnes
   410 East 62nd Street
   New York, New York
Private residence
Location: Mt. Desert Island, Maine
Engineers:
   Severud-Perrone-Sturm-Bandel (structural)
   Robert K. Bedell (mechanical)
Contractor: Horace Bucklin
Photographer: David Franzen

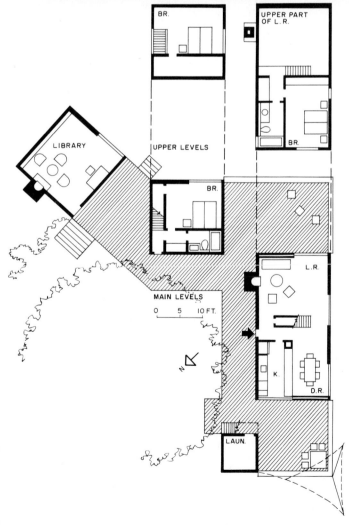

7:

When the architect and owners first explored the possibilities for this densely-wooded, 150-acre site, a "tree-house" with expansive outdoor decks seemed a reasonable starting point for conceptual design. As the functional requirements became clearer and more precisely defined, the tree house notion was modified to a more conventional elevated platform structure, but the broad areas of deck remained and a sense of living among the trees persisted as an important design theme.

The primary spaces in the house are grouped into two wings—one for parents, one for offspring—and in each case, vertical zoning places sleeping areas above living areas (see plans, page 120). The two wings are linked by a short, glass-enclosed bridge. Openings, as well as decks, are oriented toward handsome views of three man-made lakes that change their aspect both by time of day and season. A fourth lake lies out of sight from the house a quarter mile to the west. The rest of the property is heavily wooded, giving the house an unusual degree of isolation and a special sense of its own privacy.

The enrichment of the simple cube forms by careful, knife-edged additions and subtractions, the consistency of the white-painted plywood exterior and the detachment of the whole mass from the earth plane combine to make this house stand apart from its natural surroundings—not in conflict with them, but in sharply focused contrast.

Architects: Don Hisaka & Associates
  project architect: George Saire
  257 The Arcade
  Cleveland, Ohio
Private residence
Location: Northern Ohio
Engineers:
  Gensert-Peller Associates (structural)
  George Evans & Associates (mechanical)
  Lombardi & Associates (electrical)
Contractor: Buell Davidson
Photographer: Thom Abel

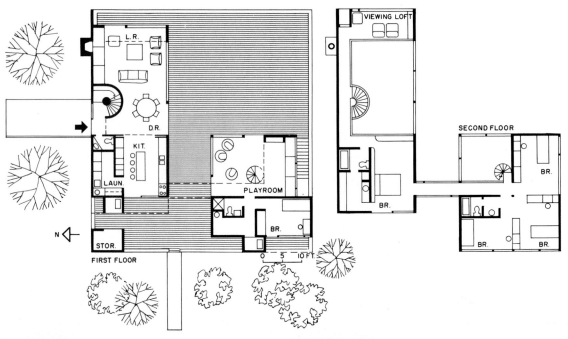

VIEWING LOFT

SECOND FLOOR

L.R.

D.R.

KIT.

LAUN.

PLAYROOM

BR.

STOR.

BR.

BR.

BR.

BR.

FIRST FLOOR

N

0   5   10 FT.

8: When the owners leave their suburban home on summer weekends, they retreat to this unorthodox vacation house perched atop a Cape Cod hill. "Like a ship floating on the land" is how the architect Giovanni Pasanella's associate, Thea Kramer, describes the house, and the analogy is a good one. The hilltop site is flat, and, except for sand formations, scrub pines and other hardy flora, totally undistinguished. But the views—of the sea, a salt marsh, and a distant town—are great, and varied in all directions. No building is close by. By breaking up the usual four-square box to create many viewing angles (both through and out the house), the architect reasoned that he could take best advantage of the site, while still organizing the house for the owner's practical requirement: "an economical, varied space for themselves and guests to feel comfortable together or alone." The family includes a teenaged son and daughter, and separation of their activities was required.

Spaces and shapes lend this house its perennial vacation air of built-in delight and relaxation. It is a vacation environment—though equipped

with space heating and all amenities for year-round use and planned with a realistic eye.

To take best advantage of the view, the usual multi-level house plan has been reversed, with major living areas open to major views on the second floor, and chil-dren's and guest bedrooms a few steps below the first, or entry, floor. Master bedroom is on the third. By going up instead of out, and by placing main glass areas clear of the ground, the house can be totally buttoned up, and is worry free for the owners when away.

Architect: GIOVANNI PASANELLA
154 West 57th Street, New York City
Etel Thea Kramer, associate architect
Owners: Dr. and Mrs. Alan Grey
Location: Wellfleet, Massachusetts
Structural engineer: Stanley Gleit
Contractor: Allen Jordan

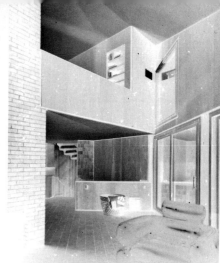

Weathered white cedar shingles and corner board windows are pure Cape Cod vernacular and picked because they make good sense. Decks (photo above) are off master bedroom; (below) off livingroom on second floor. Lower level bedroom windows peer through cedar trees close by. Entry leads to low-ceilinged hall (above), open to kitchen above, and yellow enameled cast iron spiral stair. Seemingly complex, the house was designed by juxtaposing two squares, then removing triangular volumes (for decks, pitched roof) as it goes up. House has concrete block foundation to anchor it to the ground, virtually composed of shifting sand.

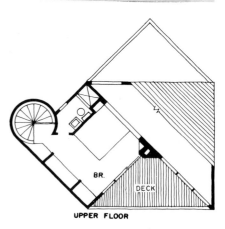

UPPER FLOOR

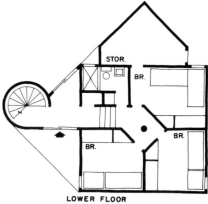

LOWER FLOOR

David Hirsch photos

View (left above) is master bedroom, overlooking livingroom and opening to its own deck, which, in turn, overlooks livingroom (left below). Walls are cedar plywood; exposed structure is enameled a deep red. Exposed framing painted as trim helped account for total $27,000 cost. Play of space is stabilized by warm red tones and the orientation stair and fireplace provide.

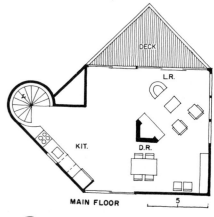

MAIN FLOOR   5

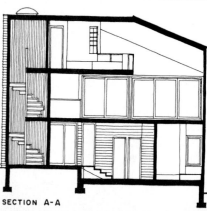

SECTION A-A

9:

This house on the sparsely settled north coast of California is both a weekend and vacation house for its owners and a retreat for longer periods from their small flat on Telegraph Hill in San Francisco, an hour's drive away. The site is a 60- by 450-foot plot, at the base of the coast range, with an unobstructed view of the ocean from the front and of the 2000-foot ridge, half a mile inland, from the back. All the principal spaces have one or the other of these views.

Since the owners spend much of their time at the beach outdoors, the house is also planned for a free and casual relationship between interior and exterior spaces. In contrast to the open terraces on both ocean and ridge sides of the house, the patio is a carefully controlled exterior environment, enclosed by two pairs of high gates, front and back, between the house and the studio block, which give privacy and protection from the strong winds of this section of the coast. Within the 24- by 24-foot patio, plants provide seasonal color and variety of texture: outside the patio, beach grass is allowed to grow up to the house. A vegetable garden is located behind the house. The house is in two parts—living spaces in the main building, two studio workshops in a separate structure. The living-dining-kitchen area is designed to a scale that is comfortable for two people or, on occasion, for a larger number of people. Essentially, these two parts are boxes whose volumes are controlled by the dimensions of the resawn-redwood plywood panels (10 foot, standard, with grooves 4 inches apart) used throughout. Details are consistent: standard sliding residential door units connect major rooms and patio; exterior trim is all-heart solid redwood; the roof structure is a system of beams and decking, and the same trim is used at the termination of the sheetrock wall finish just below the roof framing; interiors are painted all white.

Architect: Morton Rader
  of Chan/Rader & Associates
  710 Sansome Street
  San Francisco, California
Private residence
Location: Marin County, California
Engineers:
  Stefan Medwadowski (structural)
  Charles & Braun and
  Montgomery & Roberts (mechanical)
  Mazzetti & Parish (electrical)
Interior and landscape design:
  Morton Rader and Betty Bird
Contractors: Edward W. Burger, Inc.
Photographer: Bernard Poinssot

The patio is the heart of the house and its carefully controlled environment
is regulated by the high gates, at front and rear, which provide for privacy
or open to the views to ocean and ridge, and protect from wind.

The interior spaces are small but seem large, thanks to the open relationship between them, and to the unifying effect of the all-white walls and ceilings. All major rooms open to views, either to the ocean or to the high ridge inland that runs parallel to the beach, and to the patio whose environment, visually and climatically protected, allows use in all but stormy weather. The restrictions imposed by a modest budget, handled with skill and grace, are incorporated into the design as elements of it.

10:

A house on the meadow at the Sea Ranch is a highly visible object, exposed to view from the hills and from the highway that separates meadow and hills. In such an open landscape, the size, form and color of a building are unusually important since they determine the degree of contrast between building and land.

The two buildings that make up this unpretentious weekend house are simple in form and color, and, in their straightforward use of rough-sawn stained wood, have the pleasant indigenous look of an old weathered barn. The smaller of the two buildings, now used as a studio-study and a garage, served as living quarters while the main building was under construction. The two principal requirements of the clients were simplicity and privacy for themselves and their three teenage children. Locating the bedrooms at either end of the big

room was a logical—though to the clients, unconventional—way of obtaining privacy, but the clients readily accepted it and found that it worked out well not only for the family but when the house is rented, as it often is, since two couples can occupy it and still have privacy. Guests are provided for in the main building; for an overflow number, window seats convert to bunks, and an aerie above one of the bedrooms can be used for sleeping. The big room, with a view to the ocean at one end and an open kitchen at the other, is the gathering place for everyone. With commendable understanding of the character of the place, the owners have allowed the indigenous wild grasses to grow up to the buildings.

RESIDENCE FOR GLEN NIMNICHT, The Sea Ranch, California. Architect: *Fred L. Osmon.* Engineer: *Harold Davis* (structural). Contractor: *Rick Gladjo.*

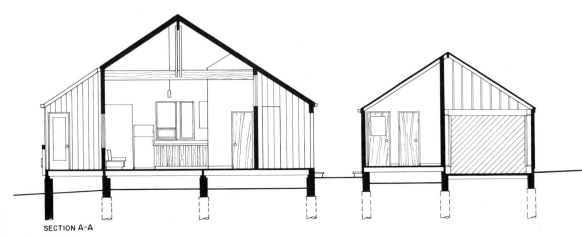

SECTION A-A

Merg Ross photos

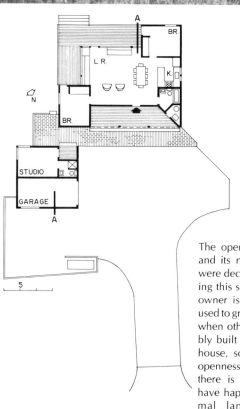

The openness of the meadow and its nearness to the ocean were deciding factors in selecting this site for the house. (The owner is from Wyoming, and used to great open spaces.) Even when other houses are inevitably built around and near this house, some of the feeling of openness will survive because there is no break—as would have happened with more formal landscaping—between house and land. The wide deck on two sides of the big room is directly accessible from both bedrooms as well as from the living room. The high ceiling over the big room is wood sheathed; dry wall is used for interior partitions.

131

11:

A simply-constructed wood barrel vault transforms this straightforward post-and-beam vacation house into an elegant residence. Perched above a rambling creek near Wausa, Nebraska, the $20,000 building by architect Neil Astle makes use of folding doors to provide a maximum of five sleeping rooms. Triple 2 by 12 Western red cedar beams running the long dimension of the house as floor structure, both ways as roof structure, and supported by columns made up of two 2 by 10s and a 2 by 8 spacer, form the basic grid. Two-by-six decking is used on both roof and walls to enclose it.

The four semi-circular trusses which form the 15-foot diameter barrel vault (left) also use 2 by 12s. The paired curved sections cut from them have a two layer inner core of ¾-inch fir plywood all of which is glued (with exterior glue) and nailed together. All joints are carefully staggered; the semi-circular elements are braced by a double 2 by 12 bottom chord and a kingpost of 2 by 4s either side of a center 2 by 2 that interlocks top and bottom. Four-ply built-up roofing is used everywhere topped with gravel on the flat portion and roll roofing on the vault. A similar arched pergola of spaced 4 by 4s over the deck is planned for the future to deal with glare from the sky.

Architect: NEIL ASTLE of Neil Astle and Associates. *Owner:* Dr. and Mrs. R. L. Tollefson. *Location:* Wausa, Nebraska. *Engineer:* Robert Sullivan (mechanical). *Carpentry contractor:* Arnold Prather.

133

12:

Architect Alfredo DeVido's houses have a freshness in their massing, a no-nonsense approach to detailing and a low-maintenance character in the selection of their finishes. The Sheehy house in eastern Long Island is not an exception. The owners, who have three children, wanted some separation between children and parent areas and asked specifically for a dining alcove off the living room. The zoning was accomplished by creating a separate children's bedroom block linked to the main portion of the house by a second-story bridge. Under the bridge, DeVido has developed a deck that serves chiefly as recreational space off the lower-level playroom. The remainder of the plan is tightly organized around a central stair and chimney. The double-height living room opens in two directions to provide views of the site, which is covered by a stand of pines. A small outdoor deck, a portion of it covered over (top photo), extends the living room out into the site, and provides a sunny and sequestered corner for outdoor activity.

With ease of upkeep and his client's budget in mind, DeVido kept the framing in simple box-like forms, departing from this vocabulary only as necessary to create a stair that is expressed on the outside wall of the children's wing (photo below). Materials, too, have been selected for easy maintenance: tile for floors, painted stucco for the chimney, unpainted wood siding for walls and partitions inside and out.

The Sheehy house, though unselfconscious and not visibly overconcerned about style, is nonetheless strongly composed, carefully proportioned and comfortably furnished. To its credit, it accomplishes just what it sets out to do—with little or no wasted motion or unwelcome posturing.

Architect: Alfredo DeVido
    27 West 53rd Street
    New York, New York
Owners: Mr. and Mrs. John Sheehy
Location: Long Island, New York
Engineers: Charles Thornton (structural)
    Fred Weber (mechanical)
Contractor: Henry Dankowski
Photographer: Bill Maris

SECOND FLOOR

BR. BR. BR. OPEN TO L.R.

PLAYRM. U K. D.R. L.R.

FIRST FLOOR

N

5

The canted skylight (above right) occurs over the master bedroom, which in turn overlooks the living room through a three-window port (photos above). The kitchen (at right) forms an "L" between the dining room and outdoor deck, positioned so that it can serve both of these spaces directly.

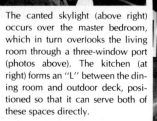

13:

On the hills at Sea Ranch, most house sites are out of view among trees and bushes, although some—on the slope of the hill facing the ocean—are in plain view of the meadow. Up on the hill, however, sites tend to be shady, with sunlight filtered through the trees, so that daylight in the houses must be designed for. Since houses on the hill are so little exposed to general view—in contrast to those on the meadow—forms are often more complex. The overriding character is, nevertheless, simple. The owners of this house, a retired couple, had lived for several years at the Sea Ranch in one of the "Binker Barns" designed by William Turnbull and Charles Moore (RECORD HOUSES of 1973, pages 74-5), and had learned to know and appreciate the exceptional quality of the original Sea Ranch buildings and to want the same quality in their new house. The house is simple and unpretentious, reminiscent of the Sea Ranch vernacular but individual in its handling of details and forms. The sloping site allowed for placement of garage, shop and storage under the main house with a minimum disturbance of grade. This gives living areas just enough elevation to afford some view of Black Point and the ocean and, through the trees, of a meadow on the south. Guest rooms are separate from the main house in a compact and appropriately simple unit on the same level as the house. The main living space is open and light, with large windows on two sides and additional light from a monitor window above.

RESIDENCE FOR MR. AND MRS. HENRY O. WHITESIDE, The Sea Ranch, California. Architect: *Donald Jacobs*. Contractor: *Custom Builders, Inc.*

DINING ROOM   ENTRY

GARAGE

SECTION A-A   5

MAIN LEVEL
5

L.R.   D.R.   KIT.

UTIL.

BR.

BR.

BR.

STOR   SHOP

GARAGE

LOWER LEVEL

The sculptural forms of the charred remains of old tree stumps, retained and incorporated into the design, are a feature of the entrance to the house. Logs of various lengths, set vertically beside steps from driveway to entrance, further emphasize the woody character of the place. Very few living trees were removed to make way for the house, so during most of the day, sunlight reaches the house through the trees. To bring in as much daylight as possible to entry and dining area, a kind of "light tower" was placed over the entry (across page, top and bottom). Light from its high monitor window (see section) bounces against the opposite wall and ricochets across to dining area.

Merg Ross photos

141

Despite its essentially shady location, the house gets plenty of light, thanks to the openness of the plan—which makes one big room of living, dining and kitchen spaces—and to the skylights over kitchen and utility room (right: seen from entry) and the monitor window (see section, page 140) which supplement the large windows on the south and west. The sunny deck (below) opens off the living room and has maximum exposure to what sun is available.

Norman McGrath photos

14:

There is a strength and majesty to the granite seawall of Maine that makes it impossible for any work of man to dominate—or indeed try to compete. Wisely, architect Robert Burley has chosen to site this house so that a high lip of rock at the top of the promontory shields the house and acts as a "railing," and so that a few trees soften the stark and beautiful views. Because of its siting, its shape, and its white cedar finish, the house is hardly visible from offshore.

While at first glance this house appears simple and subdued, it is full of visual surprises—changes of scale and heights, unexpected views, and a thoroughly pleasant plan that must be a joy to live with.

In concept, the house is a fragmented pyramid (see roof plan, near right) pulled apart into four cedar-shingled blocks with tall, glass-walled galleries separating each one. The pitched roofs and fragmented character bear a strong relationship, again, to the site; and the cedar shingle exterior and edge-grain fir interior give the house a quiet consistency that sets off (or is set off by) the dramatic site

and architectural forms of the house. Creating this quiet simplicity requires, of course, great care and skill in detailing: note the absence of fascias at the eaves, and the walls "beveled" back to the windows without apparent thickness at the corners. On the inland side, the house is approached through heavy spruce forest and the impact of the views is not felt until one has moved well into the house.

The living spaces are thoughtfully disposed into the segments of the house. From the entry (top right in plan), two broad halls or galler-

ies—both glass walled at their ends and thus offering dramatic glimpses to the forest and sea—lead to the master-bedroom suite or to the kitchen-dining pavilion. The high-ceilinged living room is entered, up four broad steps, from either gallery. Stairs in both hall wings lead to an upstairs gallery, serving a study (above the master bedroom) and a second bedroom (tucked under the roof of the kitchen-dining pavilion).

Architects: ROBERT BURLEY AS-SOCIATES. *Location:* the Maine coast. *Contractor:* E. L. Shea, Inc.

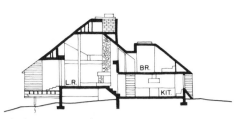

In section, the living room pavilion is raised above the main floor level to accommodate an immovable piece of the Maine shoreline which cropped up at that spot, and to give the large glass walls of the living room a clearer view to the sea. All photos show a skill in craftsmanship that is rare today—and both architect and owner are high in their praise for builder Phil Shea. Inside, all floors, ceilings, and walls are edge-grain fir panelling except for black Maine slate on the gallery level and in the kitchen. Shingles are white cedar; windows, and sliding doors are framed in bronze-finish aluminum. Roofs were truncated at the top to simplify framing, and these flat sections are metal-capped. Square footage of the house: 2,020.

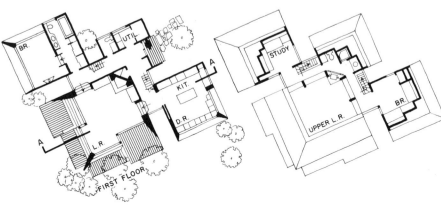

15:

This vacation house at the Sea Ranch in California is built on a heavily wooded site on a hill above Sea Ranch's well-publicized meadows. Except for one small swath cut through to allow a view of the distant ocean, the site feels private, and the windows open onto views of the adjacent trees.

Consequently the exterior of the house (photo right) has been kept as simple as possible ("You can barely see it from most directions," the architect points out), and the form, too, is nothing more than one large box with a sloping roof, with two bedroom lean-to's.

Inside, though, there are surprises. For one thing there are two large skylights in the roof above the shower room and the kitchen area (seen in the bottom photos on the opposite page). These admit not just light, but direct light into the house—moving and changing with the hour and the seasons, and contrasting with the dappled sunbeams that filter through the trees and enter through the windows.

The architect has also made a considerable point of the variety of activities and moods that can be accommodated in the one big room of his house. The toilet, for instance, is in the only space that is completely enclosed, and the guest bedroom (seen in the background of the photo below right) is, when unoccupied, open to the living area by a vertically-sliding *shoji*, and separated from the seats around the fireplace only by a *tatami* platform for sitting (without the aid of chairs) or sleeping (without beds) or for meditating.

Above the *tatami* platform are two sleeping lofts reached by a vertical ladder. They are open to the large room below, as is the bathing area (behind the wall in the bottom left photo opposite). The act of bathing is enlivened by a large wooden Japanese bathtub, by a shower and by a view from the shower room to the outside, through sliding glass doors that open onto a deck.

With all these blandishments the house invites the joyful liberations of vacation-house living. It even has a Moon Gate (photo right). Why? "Just because I like Moon Gates," the architect says.

Architect and owner: Dmitri Vedensky
2262 Mason Street
San Francisco, California
Location: Sea Ranch, California
Contractor: Harold Halvorsen
Photographer: Gerald K. Lee

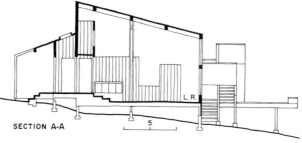

SECTION A-A

The section above shows the shape of the one large room, and of one of the bedroom lean-to's. The main entrance is on the left; decks, platforms and Moon Gate are shown on the right.

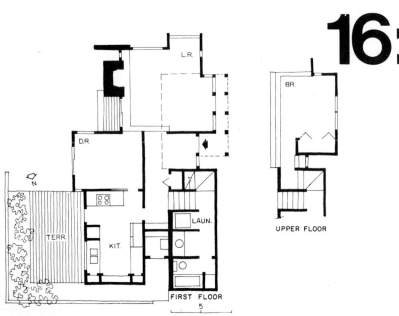

L.R.

BR.

D.R.

TERR.

KIT.

LAUN.

UPPER FLOOR

FIRST FLOOR

5

16:

It used to be that "vacation house" meant a modest cottage in a lovely spot. While none of the houses in this collection are large or pretentious, Donald Sandy's house for Mr. and Mrs. John Crossman comes closest to that simple old-fashioned idea. The plan, the form and the details all express an informality that seems appropriate for rural living. However, informality does not mean shoddy or incomplete finish. For $23,000 architect Sandy has provided interiors, above right, with walls of the same diagonal resawn redwood boards as on the exterior, oak floors and a large fireplace of field stone found on the site. The massive chimney provides important shear resistance to the Pacific Ocean winds, which were carefully charted when Sea Ranch was conceived and which have contributed a groundhugging silhouette to this house and others built there. A future bedroom addition will supplement the sleeping loft which has a unique floor structure of laminated 2x4s.

Location: Sea Ranch, Sonoma County, California. Owners: *Mr. and Mrs. John Crossman*; architect: *Donald Sandy, Jr.*; contractor: *Bill Pauley*.

Joshua Freiwald photos

17:

A. Youngmeister photos

This ingenious vacation house has been built well over a dozen times at the Sea Ranch in California. The basic notion is simplicity itself: a barn-like space with a plan that can be flipped and with an appended lean-to whose function is variable. The working out of the notion, though, assures that simplicity does not lead to dullness.

The ground floor plan is circuitous, so that the apparent size of the space is increased because the eye can never see all of it at once. The "Z" shaped plan of the second floor allows sunlight to fall into the living areas from skylights in the roof, casting patterns that change with the hours and the seasons. It also provides upward vistas from below, and the pleasure of moving from a low space, like the dining area, to one that is dramatically higher. One can also move outside the enclosing walls of the house to lounge in a bay window, or right up to the peak of the roof to doze or sleep in one of the lofts there. What begins, then, as a simple space ends up providing an admirable array of different places to be and things to do.

The architects assumed that in a vacation house choices of what to do and where to do it would be made casually, and so the feeling of the interior is relaxed. The details are simple, the rough-sawn boards are left unfinished, and the heavy framing members stand fully exposed.

Outside, this way of building produces an effect that is downright modest, recalling simple rural structures. It has turned out that, at the Sea Ranch, this assumption of modesty was wise, for as more and more houses are built on the open meadows, each more obviously "designed" than the next, and each one competing with all the others for attention, there is the danger that the place may begin to look more like a statuary farm than the beautifully desolate landscape which it once was, and which the original developers, planners and architects had sought with great care to preserve.

PRIVATE RESIDENCE, The Sea Ranch, California. Architects: *William Turnbull and Charles Moore of MLTW / Moore-Turnbull; Robert Theel,* associate. Engineers: *Patrick Morreau* (structural); *Brelje and Race* (civil). Contractor: *Matthew D. Sylvia.*

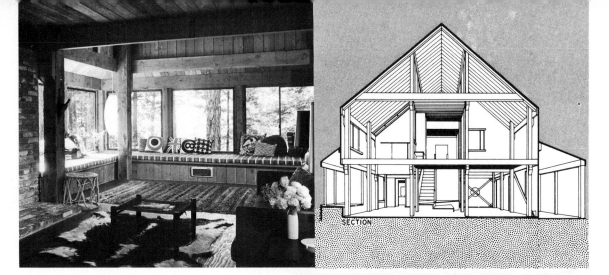

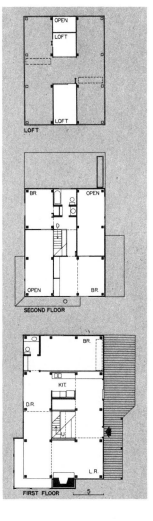

The "Blinker Barn," named for the salesman who came up with the idea, is repeatable in several different versions. The basic shape is a heavy-framed box, with a kitchen and living areas on the first floor, two bedrooms and a bath above, and, higher still, lofts for sleeping, or simply for retreat. The lean-to can be a carport, a garage, or a third bedroom with bath. Or a separate garage can be added.

18:

For all its quiet, woodsy appearance on the exterior, the rooms within this summer and weekend house have been created with an unusually bold and sophisticated exuberance. Varied ceiling heights and slopes, balconies, overlooks and peek-throughs, and changes in floor levels—all abound to form an environment full of civilized fun.

The house is wood framed and clad in western red cedar siding and terne roofs. Though some interior surfaces are painted dry wall panels, many of the walls and most of the ceilings are of oak. Floors are brick, oak or quarry tile.

The main level of the house is a fairly open plan, but the spaces delineated by the floor and ceiling level changes range from the bright openness of the two-story living room to the snug cozyness of the central dining space. One stair to the upper

level is detached in a sort of service tower and provides quick access to the bedrooms and study which occupy all of one second floor wing. It is connected to the master bedroom wing (an extensive suite of bedroom, with a sitting area by a fireplace, porch, and two large dressing rooms) by a bridge running through the living area.

Decks—some open, some covered and one screened—surround most of the main floor level and provide as remarkable a variety of sunny or shady nooks and sitting areas as do the rooms on the interior.

Architect: HARRY C. WOLF of Wolf, Johnson & Associates
213 Latta Arcade, Charlotte, North Carolina
M. P. Carroll, associate-in-charge
Mountain Residence
Location: Western North Carolina
Engineers: R. V. Wasdell & Associates; John Bolen Associates; S. C. Wilber
Interior design: Wolf Associates, R. G. Kromelow
Contractor: Blythe and Isenhour, Inc.

SECTION A-A

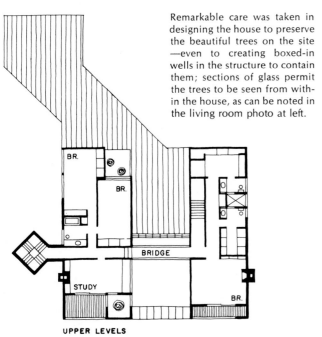

Remarkable care was taken in designing the house to preserve the beautiful trees on the site —even to creating boxed-in wells in the structure to contain them; sections of glass permit the trees to be seen from within the house, as can be noted in the living room photo at left.

BR.

BR.

BRIDGE

STUDY

BR.

UPPER LEVELS

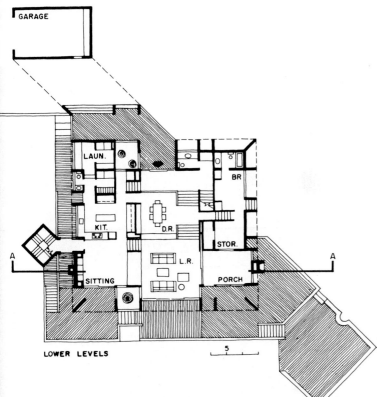

GARAGE

LAUN.

BR.

KIT.

D.R.

STOR.

A

A

L.R.

SITTING

PORCH

LOWER LEVELS

5

19:

Truro is a small community located near the northern tip of Cape Cod. The peninsula narrows abruptly near Truro to a minimum width of half a mile, granting many residents views of both the ocean and the bay. The land is tufted with scrub pine and pocked by small glacial basins.

This summer house for a minister and his family, designed by architect Paul Krueger, stands at the lip of one such basin and steps down into its depth to provide a measure of privacy for the lower level bedroom. A twelve-foot-wide, three-level volume, the house is framed in tripled 2 by 12s diagonally braced at top and bottom. Additional bracing—against high winds—is provided by external guy wires turnbuckled to "dead men" at either side of the house (see photo right).

Built on an extraordinarily modest construction budget (under $12,000), the house is clad in cedar board and batten, exposed on the exterior, and joined to the main vertical structure by horizontal nailers. Floors are fir decking and the roof is finished in cedar shingle. Minimum enclosure, simple construction, minor requirements for equipment, and the sparing use of interior finishes kept costs at rock bottom. But in spite of these economies, the Mark house has a freshness and inventiveness that derives from its siting and the playfulness of its forms. The interior spaces open outward and upward to expand the 12-foot-width and provide easy avenues of visual release. Inside and out, the house has a consistent vocabulary of details and a pleasant sense of leisure and relaxed informality. It is a house where wet bathing suits do not seem out of place.

Future plans include a small bedroom wing to be constructed farther down the slope and attached to the main structure by a stepped bridge. When the addition is complete, the existing lower level bedroom will become a family room.

Architect: PAUL H. KRUEGER. Associate architect: Malcolm Montague Davis. *Owner:* Reverend and Mrs. Edward L. Mark. *Location:* Truro, Massachusetts. *Structural engineers:* Tsaing Engineering; *structural consultant:* Souza and True. *Contractor:* Colp Brothers.

The approach to the house is a 12-foot-wide bridge-deck that provides a pleasant, sequestered setting for outdoor dining. It also introduces a design theme that will be expanded when the planned bedroom wing is added farther down the basin.

The architect had hoped to expose the braced structure over the roof but was barred from doing so by local code.

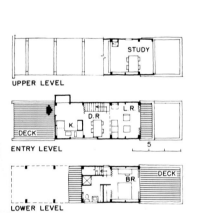

UPPER LEVEL

ENTRY LEVEL

LOWER LEVEL

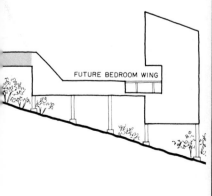

FUTURE BEDROOM WING

Steve Rosenthal photos

Thirteen beach houses

1: The strong, contained forms of this beach house reflect a remarkable arrangement of interior spaces within—many levels to effectively zone the house into activity areas, and windows unusually placed to provide panoramic, and sometimes unexpected views. The basic shape of the house is consciously geared to its site. Architect Jaffe comments that, "the site is a dune, a capricious cross section of sand meeting water, subject to the winds and the shifting of the tides. The shape of the dune is permissive, demanding a structure with a stance of its own: the 'feet' of the house are column extensions of wooden piles driven to below sea level on the land side of the dune; the columns continue up to become a roof returning to overhang the openings facing the ocean; the roof on the land side turns downward echoing the sliding return of the dune."

All this is sheathed—roof and walls—in cedar shakes, which helps to both unify and dramatize the sculptural qualities of the protrusions and insets of the design. To anchor the house solidly to its site, rough-hewn granite is used as a podium, extended to form an entrance court and retaining wall for the living room terrace at the top of the dune (see photos at left and below).

The lowest of the levels which zone the house contains the entry and childrens' rooms. The latter have a separate entrance and little terrace on the east facade of the house (photo bottom left). A freestanding stair leads up one-half level to an area for guests, with bedroom, studio and bath. Spiraling above this are the living areas (living room, dining room, kitchen and gallery), each of which are a few steps above the other. The top level or zone contains the master bedroom, studio, master bath, and a deck which cantilevers over the crest of the dune (photos below).

Very out-of-the-ordinary windows are used to give daylight and good views to this rising succession of spaces. At the front of the house, a large window is notched into the facade to give a long down-slope vista from the main stair, and another window/skylight is set into front wall and roof to give sky views and light to both a guest room (photo below center) and to the higher-level gallery leading to the master bedroom floor (see section overleaf). Extra light is given to the gallery by a long skylight over the living room (see photo below). The main living rooms have wide banks of sliding glass walls facing the ocean, as does the master bedroom. The latter also has a little window to the east for view and morning sun.

The combination of the unusually placed and sized windows, the projections of the various cantilevers, and the skin-like "wrapping" of cedar shakes give the relatively small house an arresting, and eye-deceiving sense of monumental scale without compromise to its overall sense of warmth and comfort.

Architect: NORMAN JAFFE 125 East 80th Street, New York, New York. *Associate:* Michael Wolfe. *Owners:* Mr. and Mrs. Stephen Perlbinder. *Location:* Sagaponac, Long Island, New York. *Structural engineer:* James Romeo. *Contractor:* Stephen Perlbinder

The small photos above show the effect from inside the house of some of the unorthodox windows. At left is a little room on the guest level which is roofed by a window skylight. The master bedroom (above) has both views and sense of seclusion.

A

B

C

Bill Maris photos

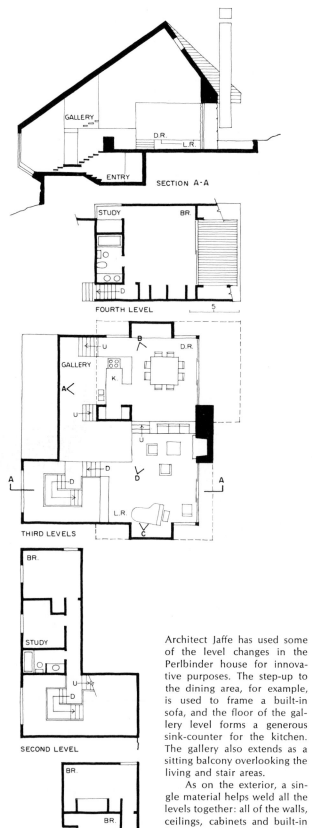

GALLERY

D.R.
L.R.

ENTRY   SECTION A-A

STUDY   BR.

D

FOURTH LEVEL   5

U   B   D.R.

GALLERY

A   K.

U

U

D   D
D

A   A

L.R.

C

THIRD LEVELS

BR.

STUDY

U
D

SECOND LEVEL

BR.

BR.

N   U

FIRST LEVEL

Architect Jaffe has used some of the level changes in the Perlbinder house for innovative purposes. The step-up to the dining area, for example, is used to frame a built-in sofa, and the floor of the gallery level forms a generous sink-counter for the kitchen. The gallery also extends as a sitting balcony overlooking the living and stair areas.

As on the exterior, a single material helps weld all the levels together: all of the walls, ceilings, cabinets and built-in furniture are Douglas fir, and the floors are either of the same material or of Pennsylvania slate.

D

Norman McGrath

2:

This vacation house in eastern Long Island stands on a high point of ground surrounded by dense shrubbery and overlooking both the ocean and the town of Montauk. Both the owners, Mr. and Mrs. Peter Lowenstein, and the architects Chimacoff/Peterson, share a preference for simple geometric forms and neither wished to thrust aggressive shapes into this gentle landscape. The resulting design, therefore, is a simple prismatic volume of 900 square feet enclosed in a framework created by extending the exterior columns and joists to points of intersection. The larger

envelope embraces a deck, gives the whole composition an exciting transparency, and prints the solid walls with a changing abstract of cast shadows.

The south elevation (above) faces the ocean and will be fitted with adjustable canvas blinds to control the sun and glare. Just off the deck is a small grass plateau, formed by fill from the excavations, where badminton and volleyball are regularly played as part of the summer routine. At the open west end of the house (photo top), a series of observation and sunbathing platforms can be reached by

retractable ladders. Living, dining and kitchen areas share the deck level with a small guest room. A bath and two bedrooms—one overlooking the living area—occupy the upper level.

Standard materials and construction techniques have been used throughout. Exterior wall surfaces are painted plywood used, when possible, in full 4-by-8-foot sheets and put in place without battens but spaced apart by strips of flashing that give the narrow reveals a visual emphasis (see detail opposite page). Construction costs for this house were just under $40,000.

What is most appealing about the Lowenstein house is the degree of interest and spatial liveliness it generates within a carefully ordered and economic building system. Also noteworthy is the rapport the architects have established between house and site, a rapport that results from a conscious effort to place two different elements in amicable contrast.

Architects: CHIMACOFF/PETERSON. *Owner:* Mr. and Mrs. Peter Lowenstein. *Location:* Montauk, Long Island, New York. *Structural consultant:* Donald P. Greenberg. *Contractor:* David Webb.

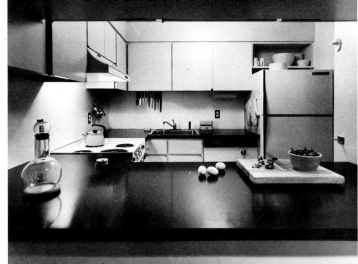

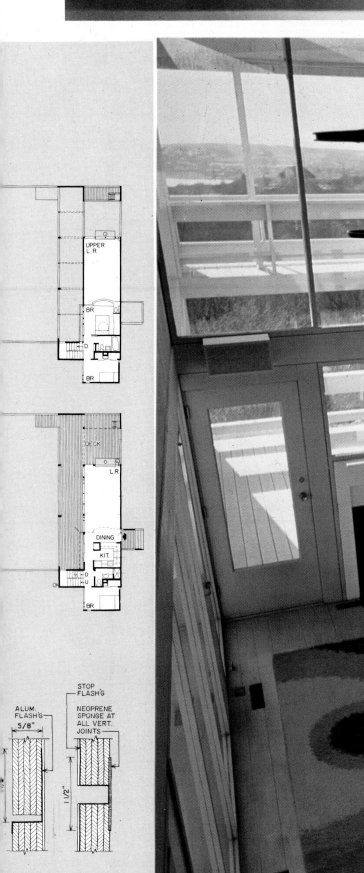

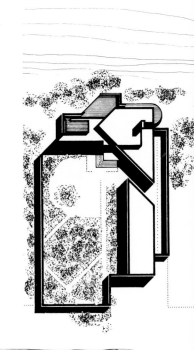

3: Architect Carl Abbott has designed an informal beach house on the Gulf of Mexico that also wraps around a lush tropical garden on the side away from the water. The main portion of the house, which is the winter residence of a New York couple who would rather be outside than in, is a raised platform for a better view of both the Gulf and the garden. It contains living rooms, the master bedroom and decks on every side. A second building, for frequent family visitors, is set in the garden itself and tied to the larger one by the stuccoed masonry walls that almost completely surround the complex.

Architect: Carl Abbott. *Owners:* Mr. and Mrs. David Weld. *Location:* an island near Sarasota, Florida. *Structural consultant:* A. L. Conyers. *Contractor:* W. C. Beall and Associates, Inc., Dale Pierce partner-in-charge.

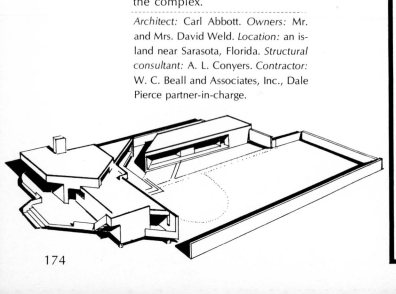

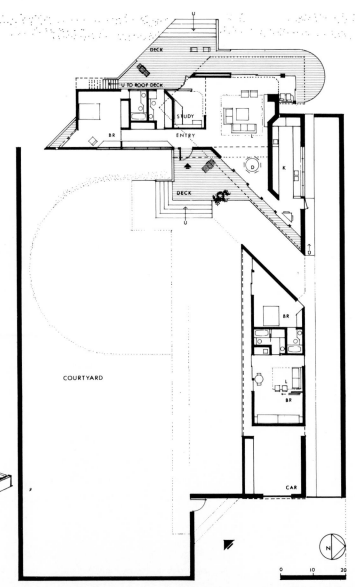

BEACH

MAIN HOUSE

GUEST HOUSE

COURTYARD

CAR

0   10   20

The living room and master bedroom (above) have views up and down the beach to the ends of the island as well as those of spectacular sun directly across the water. Horizontal rough cedar boards left to weather combined with the diagonal geometry give the house a rambling "beach shack" quality that is a surprising contrast to the more formal interior. During the day, light pours into the living room through the clerestory. At night (below), cove lighting echoes the natural effect.

4:

From the first approach by car the way is, literally, circuitous; it presents sequential views of clusters and great gatherings of trees, of the sea and finally of the front door of the main house (bottom photo, p. 178). The more public rooms of the house are spaces peculiarly configured and assembled, sometimes high, sometimes low, sometimes opening to the sea, sometimes turning away to the patio and pool behind. The plans below show that long diagonal vistas are provided through all this complexity, anchoring axes that give the inhabi-

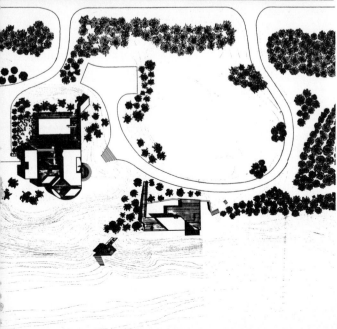

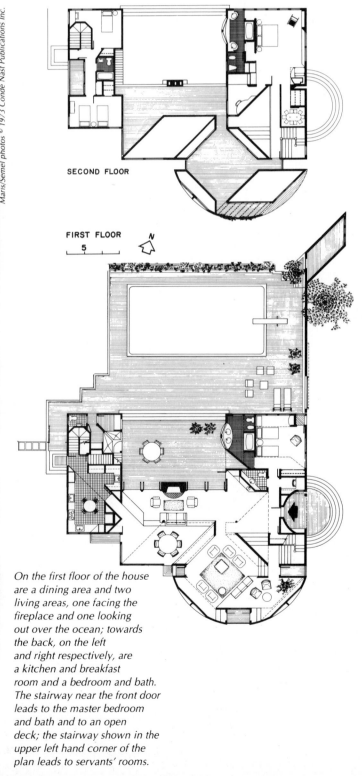

SECOND FLOOR

FIRST FLOOR   N
5

On the first floor of the house
are a dining area and two
living areas, one facing the
fireplace and one looking
out over the ocean; towards
the back, on the left
and right respectively, are
a kitchen and breakfast
room and a bedroom and bath.
The stairway near the front door
leads to the master bedroom
and bath and to an open
deck; the stairway shown in the
upper left hand corner of the
plan leads to servants' rooms.

tants some sense of the whole from any one part. The complex order of the house is thus revealed by these swaths which cut through the inside.

Faint memories of old beach houses on the Atlantic are evoked on the outside by the cedar shingles and on the inside by the old-fashioned, consciously clumsy brick fireplace (below center). Memories are evoked, too, by the surfaces of the walls and ceilings, made from narrow tongue and groove boards with half-round beadings at their joints—the kind that used to be used for wainscoting, or for porch ceilings, now available (but not used here) in plastic.

With these elements of recall, with its light and airy spaces and with its handsome contemporary furnishings and bright colors, the house is a complicated potpourri of the old and the new, allying itself exclusively with neither, but to the needs and dreams of its owners.

A little distance away from the main house is a cottage for guests (one of the owners' dreams was that guests and their children should, for certain parts of their visits, be kept at arm's length), and a little farther away still is the beach (site plan, page 177). The way that movement is organized up and down and across the site, from one part of the compound to another, is in its careful clarity not unlike that used by Philip Johnson—in an altogether different idiom—for his own glass and brick houses and other buildings in New Canaan, Connecticut. At these houses on Long Island one moves from the front door of the main house down across a grassy lawn and a short wooden bridge towards the guest house, which from this vantage seems as much sundeck as house (top left); once there one has the choice of going into the house down a flight of steps or else the choice of continuing down an alternate flight of steps to the beach. On what began as a spectacular but undifferentiated site, the architects have made a set of places, indoors and out, with evident relationship to each other and to the wishes of the particular people for whom the houses were made.

HOUSE ON EASTERN LONG ISLAND, New York, Architects, landscapers and interior designers: *Robert A. M. Stern and John S. Hagmann—assistants for this project: Daniel Colbert, Jeremy Lang, John Anhorn and William Parker.* Engineers: *Zoldos-Silman* (structural); *Langer/Polise* (mechanical). Consultant: *Carroll Cline* (lighting). Contractor: *Edward Pospisil & Son, Inc.*

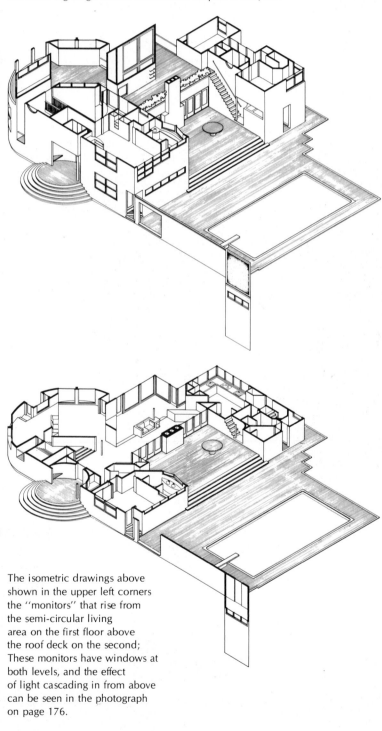

The isometric drawings above shown in the upper left corners the "monitors" that rise from the semi-circular living area on the first floor above the roof deck on the second; These monitors have windows at both levels, and the effect of light cascading in from above can be seen in the photograph on page 176.

5:

For a sandspit extending into one of Cape Cod's hundreds of fresh-water lakes, architect Earl Flansburgh has designed an assertive house of powerful imagery, complex yet beautifully ordered. From a distance across the water, the five roofs rise like a fleet of sails—surely an appropriate image for Cape Cod. You might as easily see a native village literally a step from the water—an image that begins with the roof forms and is reinforced by a "thatching" of grooved fir boards on the inside on the pyramidal roofs, by the richness and texture of materials used inside and out, and by the decks reaching out to the water's edge.

To the strong forms of the house must be added the strength of its siting: the lacing of pavilions across the spit from water's edge to water's edge is a powerful assertion of ownership.

As the plan shows, the basic concept is a series of five interconnected modules—one (the living-dining-kitchen area) larger than the others. Each is notched out under the big sheltering roofs to create a private deck, each at least partially screened. The living room has a major sunning deck on the south and east sides; opens through an all-glass wall to another major deck (foreground, photo right) facing the sunset. Thus, this main space—at any time of day—offers a choice of view, light, shade, and breeze. Each module is topped by a five-sided roof creating the large clerestories. They are carefully oriented: faced east to receive the morning sun in the master bedroom; towards the sunset in the living room.

All of the ground-level openings are double-glazed, floor-to-ceiling, and solid walls are finished in 1- by 6-inch ship-lap spruce. The roofs are shaped of yellow-pine laminated beams with concealed steel-spline joint reinforcing; supported by 8-inch-square steel-tube columns. The house has year-round heating and cooling.

Architect: Earl R. Flansburgh
   Earl R. Flansburgh and Associates
   14 Story Street
   Cambridge, Massachusetts
Owners: Mr. and Mrs. Morton Grossman
Location: Cape Cod, Massachusetts
Engineers: Souza & True (structural)
Interior design: David Millard
Landscape architects: Earl R. Flansburgh
   and Associates
Cost consultant and general contractor:
   Ely Sherman, president, Bradley
   Construction Corporation
Photographer: Steve Rosenthal

The grand living-dining-kitchen space fits under a single roof, so each area borrows space from the others. Walls are all glass for views in all directions.

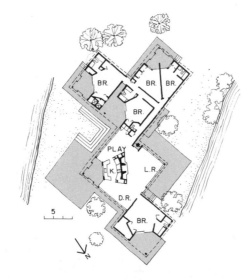

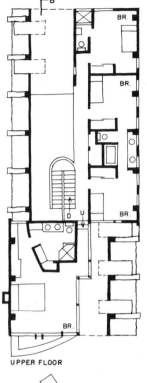

UPPER FLOOR

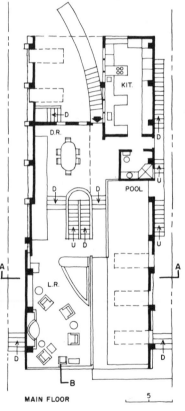

MAIN FLOOR

5

Julius Shulman photos

6: This house "goes with the waves," says architect John Lautner. Its wave-like concrete structure consists of two units of similar configuration. Each has a roof in the form of a catenary curve resting on a vertical wall. (This shape was chosen not only for visual reasons but because it puts the concrete in compression, preventing cracks.)

The units are placed against each other (photo left and section below) so that the intersecting curves expose elevations having windows. The living room and master bedroom thus gain views to the mountains as well as the beach and one of the children's rooms has a direct outlook on the ocean. This provision of light and views near the middle of the house is one of its best features. A conventional box-like structure on a lot like this one which is 37- by 110-feet would have major openings only at its ends.

The dynamism of the curved structure is reinforced by the freely composed mullions which are radial rather than grid-like in emphasis.

The whole structure is concrete except for bedroom partitions. The exterior is trowel-finished gunite applied to rough board forms. The floors are radiant heated.

It is remarkable that a house on such a small lot has five bedrooms. (The maid's room on the lower floor is not shown.) Each child's room has a balcony used for guests or as a sleeping loft.

The architect says this house "became not only an exceptionally free solution for the site and client but an interesting and practical potential for high density living." If similar houses were placed side by side there would be no windows looking into neighbors' windows and each house would have more light, privacy and better views.

This house looks as if it were fun for architect and client. True to good fun it is quite serious.

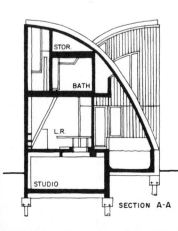

SECTION A-A

Architect: JOHN LAUTNER
7046 Hollywood Boulevard, Los Angeles, California
Owner: Mr. and Mrs. Daniel Stevens
Location: Malibu Colony, Malibu Beach, California
Structural engineer: Kamal Amin
Structural consultant: Barney Cardan
Landscape architect: Huntsman-Trout
Contractor: Paul Speer, Inc.

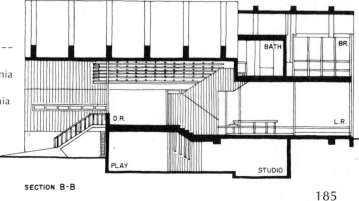

SECTION B-B

At left is the Stevens' view from the door to the 40- by 10-foot heated pool. The photo above it was taken from a similar position on the second floor overlooking the pool on the way to the master bedroom (photos top right). It has two mahogany and sail cloth fans. The larger one controls afternoon sun and the smaller one provides privacy while maintaining openness. The view from the dining room toward the living room (above) includes the cedar stairwell and baffle of the balcony corridor. The floor is impervious, matte-glazed, Japanese tile. The triangular shape in left foreground of living room (right) is open to the studio below. A slot in the roof illuminating the pool can be seen in the background.

SECOND FLOOR

FIRST FLOOR

5

7: Pajaro Dunes is a growing development of second homes near Watsonville, California overlooking Monterey Bay. Subdivision planning restricts every home to an area 50 feet square and 17 feet high. Yet within these limitations the architects solved the problems of enough space and

privacy for the clients, their three children—plus pets and frequent weekend guests— screening from adjacent neighbors, and protection from the glare—without losing the view—of the nearby ocean.

Parents' and children's bedrooms are decisively sep-

arated by an outdoor courtyard space that is sunny, wind protected, and not visible from neighboring houses, yet open to the ocean view. A big blue gable roof unites both sections of the house. The single simple form of the house as a whole sits unpretentiously among its develop-

ment neighbors, yet the playful interior contains the full array of spaces, wit and surprises for which the MLTW/ Moore Turnbull firm has earned a justifiably high reputation. The multilevel floor plan corresponds to the sand dune topography. The library, guest bedroom and entry are

Morley Baer photos

Framing of courtyard opening is part of integral structure of the house, frames the view and helps to unite the separate master bedroom wing with the rest of the house. Framing of entrance, below, formalizes the act of entering.

By running a wall to wall skylight at the edge of the roof on the ocean side of the house a substantial reduction in glare from the ocean through the view-encompassing window wall was attained. Fireplace block, containing bar, is painted with bold red design, becoming, in a way, the house's main piece of furniture.

on the lowest floor elevation, furthest from the ocean and sheltered from it by the rest of the house. The decked courtyard and immediate adjacent living room rise on a series of wide stairs, which also provide seating, to a sunny overview of a long strand of beach. Access to the second floor children's bedrooms is by way of a skylighted bridge. For the even more adventurous, a sleeping deck is carved out of the upper reaches of the master bedroom structure and is accessible from the deck by a wall-mounted ladder. The exterior is redwood boards.

Architects: CHARLES W. MOORE and WILLIAM TURNBULL, JR. of MLTW/Moore Turnbull, Pier 1½, The Embarcadero, San Francisco —Robert H. Calderwood, associate
Owners: Mr. and Mrs. John M. Naff, Jr.
Location: Pajaro Dunes, Santa Cruz County, California
Engineers: Davis & Ragsdale
Graphics designers: Jerry & Martha Wagner; Elm City Electric Light Sculpture Company
Furnishings: Ristomatti Ratia
Contractor: Richard Pollock, Pollock Construction

8:

Given the spectacular qualities of the site they possessed, these clients could hardly have selected a more capable architectural firm to design their summer home on Cape Cod than Gwathmey, Henderson, Siegel. The house, which is a piece of sculpture as well as a warm, livable and functional living unit, sits on a narrow peninsula of land jutting out into a bay where it is surrounded by a succession of beautiful views of the water. Simply because the surrounding scene was so all-encompassing and visually accessible from most of the different areas of the house, the architects purposely varied the dimensions of the view from various places in the house—creating some panoramic views and making others more selective and restrictive. At the same time all the openings are carefully related to the individual interior areas. The varying

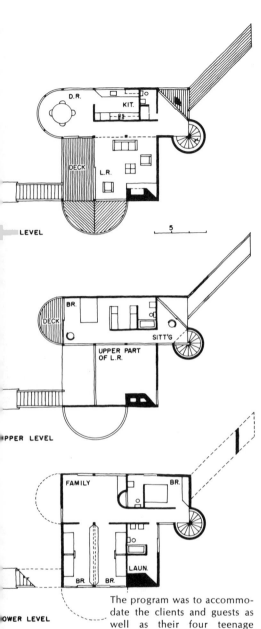

LEVEL

5

UPPER LEVEL

LOWER LEVEL

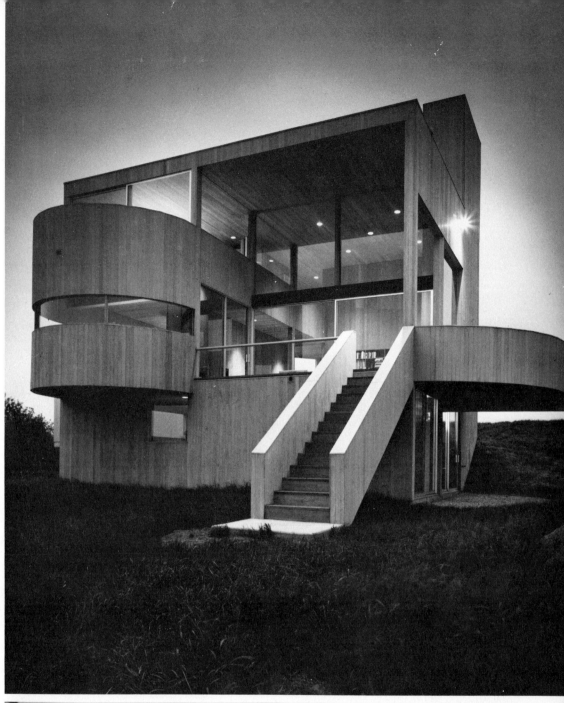

The program was to accommodate the clients and guests as well as their four teenage daughters who often have frequent weekend guests of their own. The latter problem was solved by having two bunk rooms, which sleep four people each and are separated by a storage unit, on the lower level. The girls also have their own ground level entrance. There are two other entries to the house, on the beachside by a flight of stairs to the living room deck, and by a ramp connecting main entry with parking area and garage/boat storage building (at the extreme left in photo, right).

shapes and dimensions of the generous glazed areas have another purpose as well. The architects have wedded the various spaces of the house with the space around the house via the various cutouts and openings. Two other decisions are also important factors in this particular kind of design process, which is so appropriate to a vacation house where the family spends as much time out-of-doors as inside. These are the interlocking of interior with exterior space by the use of decks, balconies and ramps which sometime jut out off the house into the surrounding space and at other times are contained in the main spatial volume as penetrations of exterior space into the house itself. The third factor is the use of the same cedar siding for both exterior and interior vertical surfaces, so that a single, unified kind of space flows in and through the house without interruption. All of these factors, of course, also give to the house its quality of a work of sculpture. The house is not just to be admired, however, it is meant to be lived in, enjoyed, and with a minimum of fuss. As is suitable to its water-surrounded site, it not

The living room, although open most of all the interior areas to the magnificent views, has a secure and sheltered feeling also, and a spaciousness all its own. View down into living room is from balcony corridor connecting upstairs study and master bedroom. While effectively sheltering its users from the wind the outside deck allows for maximum sun and with no decrease in the enjoyment of the view.

only has the look and feel of a ship but the ease of maintenance and the place-for-everything—everything-in-its-place quality of one also. Although the architects make disclaimers to any geometric or formal preconceptions, it is obvious that they favor strong and simple geometrical forms, used at their maximum effectiveness and, especially praiseworthy, assembled with maximum attention to detailing. Yet these forms, while constantly reminding us of the geometry that determines them, are also essentially functional and in keeping with the uses and activities that they contain. It would seem that uppermost in the architects' minds are spatial experiences, containment, volumes-in-space, etc. But this is never to the detriment of the more practical concerns of designing a house meant to be used as well as viewed.

Architects: CHARLES GWATHMEY, RICHARD HENDERSON and ROBERT SIEGEL of Gwathmey Henderson Siegel
210 East 86th Street, New York, New York
Owners: Mr. and Mrs. Kenneth Cooper
Location: Orleans, Massachusetts
Contractor: Anderson & Murray

Michael Zide photos

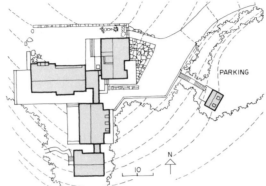

PARKING

N

10

9:

The land at Chilmark, Martha's Vineyard, swells up from the ocean in a sequence of wind-formed dunes that are stabilized precariously by wild cranberry and other low ground cover. In order to disturb this fragile site as little as possible, and to take advantage of the splendid views, architect Edward Cuetara designed this house in four functional units plus a detached studio, each supported by concrete piers, and set at various elevations dictated by the topography. A connective tissue of corridors and decks links the four units and gives the massing a deceptively unstudied and almost accidental appearance. The owners, Dr. and Mrs. William Woolner, use the house in the off-season and the division into separate units allows them to close off the guest quarters and studio to conserve heating.

To take advantage of the views, Cuetara opened the living room, bedrooms and study to the south and west. Walls turned away from the view to the north and east are mostly closed and occasionally project in the form of small sheds to house storage and other functions that do not require headroom.

The roof construction is 3-inch, laminated cedar decking that spans from the ridge beam to the outside walls. Roofing is black asphalt shingle (roll roofing on flat sections) and floors are 3-inch T & G fir plank. Inside and out, the wall finish is cedar. On the exterior, where it is licked by salt air year around, the shingle has weathered to a soft gray-brown.

More than the other houses in this collection, the Woolner residence is influenced by regional and historical traditions. The salt-box shapes, the close-in clustering of out-buildings, even the residual widow's walk (here an observation platform) pay respectful homage to this part of New England, to earlier ways and to a previous century.

WOOLNER RESIDENCE, Chilmark, Massachusetts. Owner: *Dr. & Mrs. William R. Woolner.* Architect: *Edward Cuetara.* General contractor: *Herbert R. Hancock.*

The Woolner house won a national AIA Award last year. The jury commented that the house was "a direct and convincing expression of the New England village . . . a house that fits well into the landscape without interfering with the environment." We agree.

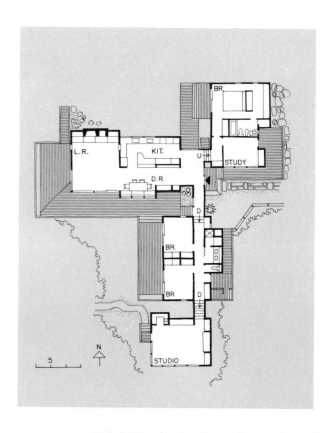

10:

Edmund Y. Lee photos

On the central Oregon coast at Salishan a beach house complex, designed by and for the architectural office of Travers/Johnston as a retreat, has been successfully created as "another world . . . a world I wish we could share with all," says Stephen Johnston. As a tribute to the delightful character of the retreat, it has been in almost constant use by the architects and employees and their families, clients and friends.

Located on the end lot of a spit of land separating Siletz Bay from the Pacific Ocean, the site has a commanding and uninterrupted 270 degree view of water. After the idea of a retreat was decided upon, the office staff was asked for suggestions with the final design concept being derived from many "bull sessions." The two major requirements were that it must be a retreat which would allow places for solitude as well as group gatherings, and that it accommodate several families at the same time. This need for a variety of spaces spurred the idea of an octagonal lodge and three hexagonal bedroom units (or modules), grouped in

a circle to create a central courtyard onto which all doors open. The focal point of the courtyard is a sunken area where guests can sit around an open fire-pit. Two decks on the ocean side provide space for sunning. A basement under one module ("Bay" on plan) serves as boat shed, laundry and storage area.

At the angles of each unit are fins extending outward. This element of the design is a strong exterior feature, visually unifying the buildings and serving as a partial windscreen against the strong and almost constant winds.

The exterior is of resawn cedar with a roof of cedar shingles. To capture the magnificent views of land and water and to allow as much light as possible to enter on the foggy and stormy days that are so much a part of the Northwest coast's weather, glass doors and many large windows are used. Glass partitions between units also serve as additional wind-screens and open up views to the courtyard. The largest of the modules, the lodge, provides such necessary community facilities as kitchen, eating and lounging areas. Smooth cedar

is used on interior walls, resawn hemlock on the ceiling. The communal character of the project is emphasized by the fact that the whole complex was not only designed but built by the architects and their staff.

BEACH HOUSE-RETREAT, Salishan, Glenedon Beach, Oregon. Architects: *Travers/Johnston.* Engineers: *MacKenzie Engineering Inc.* (structural); *Hugh L. Langton & Associates* (electrical); *McGinnis Engineering Inc.* (mechanical). Interiors: *Travers/Johnston.* Landscape architect: *William Teufel.* Contractor: *Trajon Corporation.*

An exhilarating site for a retreat, the Salishan Spit is sand dunes stabilized by pines, grasses and logs swept onto the beaches. Comprising 2000 sq ft, the retreat does not intrude on the area. The only landscaping needed was to reestablish native grasses and pines surrounding the complex.

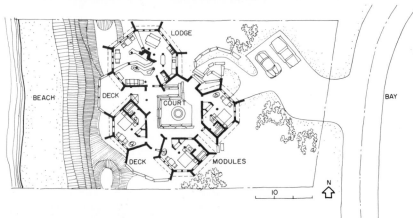

The lodge (left), as the center for most group activities, has the only kitchen, dining and lounge areas. Changes in floor level, expressed in carpet-covered concrete steps, form seating around the fire-pit and contribute to the informality of the room. The bedroom modules are identical. Two modules have views of dunes and one has an ocean view.

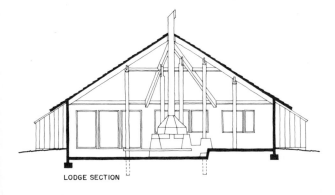

LODGE SECTION

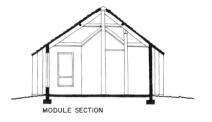

MODULE SECTION

11:

Architect Earl Combs has designed an unusual vacation house for a young family in a resort community on Long Island's South Shore. The program is hardly extraordinary but Combs has used rounded forms and symmetrical planning in ways that generate exciting spaces without producing either the inflexibility or the tormented functions that special shapes often produce.

Joseph Molitor photos

The strong circular forms of the Koplik house anchor it firmly to its site, a flat, sandy 100- by 164-foot property on Long Island's south shore. Directly across the approach road stands a tall water tower. Combs sited the house on the diagonal to avoid opening its views squarely on the tower and, in laying out the plan, the architect also strove to preserve the mask of trees that gives the house a sense of seclusion.

The paired, elongated drums (photo above), clad in vertical cedar siding, are the most conspicuous element in its massing, but the heart of the house is the double-height volume in between (see plan). Here, under a central skylight, is the space to which all the others are keyed, a living room with a built-in, circu-lar seating element facing the deck and a view through a glass wall. Flanking this space on the lower level are kitchen, dining room, maid's room, den and stair. On the level above, over-looking the living room, are three bedrooms and two baths. A bridge links the two halves of the upper level.

The curved ends of the structure have 6 ft-4 in. radii and are built using sill plates cut from 2 x 12s and fitted together to form the arc. Plywood sheathing was then nailed to wood studs and finished in cedar.

Cedar siding is also the primary finish ma-terial for walls and partitions. Floors are oak strip with polyurethane applied. The ceiling structure is exposed. Lighting is either flush-mounted or recessed incandescent throughout the house. The glazing is accomplished using stock window and door assemblies and, when these occur in rounded planes, the variable depth of the reveals seems to emphasize the roundness of the forms.

The house has some 1900 square feet of enclosed space and extends outward with decks and walks in three directions. The treat-ment of these outside spaces, though strongly geometric, seems unforced and gracious—a happy transition between the naturalness of the site and the vigorously ordered forms of the house itself.

KOPLIK RESIDENCE, Long Island, New York. Owner: *Mr. and Mrs. Michael Koplik.* Architect: *Earl Burns Combs.* Contractor: *Steven Molzon.*

The den (above) and the entryway and stair (below) are both spaces developed in the building's circular ends. The kitchen is located along an outside wall, notched for side light at the end of the counter. Bar seating provides an alternative to a more formal dining space beyond.

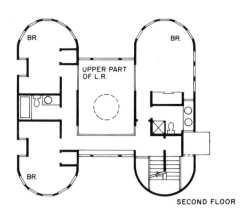

SECOND FLOOR

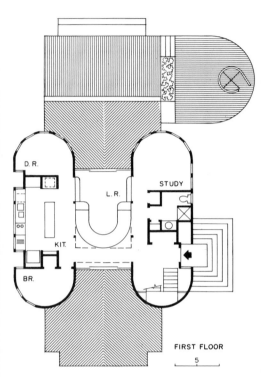

FIRST FLOOR

5

In the solid-void-solid scheme that Combs has selected for his massing, the reader might anticipate an entrance across the deck and into the central void along the axis of symmetry. Instead, Combs has created a more direct and interesting side entry (see plan above) that brings the visitor past the stair and into the central space from the back.

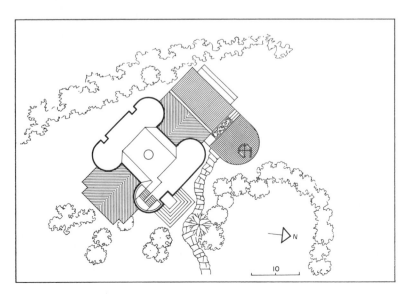

Bill Helms photos

12:

Architect Earl Combs' Fire Island beach house has a Palladian presence with its symmetry, substantiality and dominant central two-story entry way and living room. Within the overall box-like configuration this formality is reinforced by the reiteration of the square. The unglazed ceramic, mosaic tile flooring pattern is a projection of the square coffers and skylights. The columns and rooms are square, as are the basic forms of the dining and coffee tables, and the built-in seating, all designed by the architect.

Although the house is very enclosed on three sides, to assure privacy on the narrow 60- by 30-foot lot, it is actually filled with light. All rooms receive light from at least three directions. All but the living room have strip windows just below the ceiling, spanning from column to column; the baths and kitchen each has three.

The two-story skylighted living room becomes a light well for the adjoining study and dining room and the bedrooms above, which have sliding glass doors overlooking it. Mirrored sliding glass doors on the bathrooms, with their reflected views of the sea, are like internal windows. And the predominantly white floors throughout provide an additional source of reflected light. All this internal light balances glare from the beach side of the house which has floor-to-ceiling fixed glass or sliding glass doors all the way across.

Structurally the house is a variant of post and beam construction. The foundations are 6- by 6-foot posts driven 12 feet into the sand all the way down to the water. The columns are square and hollow consisting of four corner posts covered with a stiffening skin of plywood. Some columns house mechanical equipment but most are storage units provided with door panels having touch latch hardware. In the kitchen this eliminates all wall-hung cabinets, creating more open work surfaces. In the living room a four speaker sound system is built into the columns.

The ship's portholes in the bathrooms and the beach facade with deck and sunscreen resembling the bow and bridge of a ship seem quite at home next to the pounding surf.

Architect and Owner: EARL BURNS COMBS
44 West 89th Street, New York
Location: Fire Island Pines, New York
Interior Design: Earl Burns Combs
Contractor: Joseph Chasas

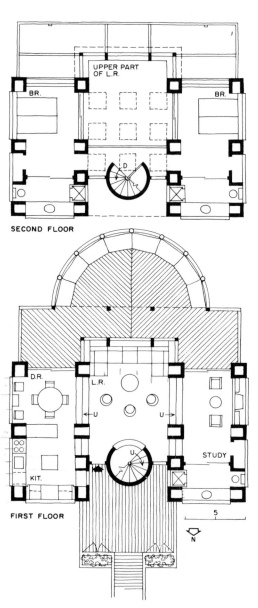

UPPER PART OF L.R.

BR.

BR.

SECOND FLOOR

D.R.

L.R.

KIT.

STUDY

FIRST FLOOR

5

N

The exterior and interior are panelled with prefinished, gray-stained plywood. Ceilings and exterior trim above the strip windows are of plastic-coated hardboard. The coffee table and built-in seating fit into the floor pattern, and the floor stripes meet and match in width the expression of the corner posts in each column, evidence of thorough detailing.

13:

A "mini-hotel," complete with sleeping for twelve, a grand staircase and a high ceilinged sitting room tucked into 1600 square feet, is the way MLTW/Turnbull Associates describe the beach house they did for a large San Francisco family. The beach front site on northern Monterey Bay has the usual problems—narrow frontage (50 ft) with undistinguished neighboring houses immediately on each side—but does face south, unusual on California's coast. It also is protected from cold northwest winds by the cliffs behind and has a view of the setting sun to the west. With their usual whimsey, the architects have turned the site and program limitations to advantage by boldly emphasizing the large amount of sleeping space required. They call the white three-story, 8-foot-wide slab in the middle of the house (left) the "sleeping machine": all the sleeping and all the machines are inside it. The shed-roofed volumes front and back are the living room and the grand staircase. The west wall of the living room (below) is angled toward the setting sun and to screen the adjacent deck from wind. In addition to many built-in items which they designed, the architects chose all furnishings for the house.

Architects: WILLIAM TURNBULL, JR. and RICHARD GARLINGHOUSE of MLTW/Turnbull Associates. *Location:* Aptos, California. *Engineers:* Hirsch and Grey (structural); Gribaldo, Jones and Associates (foundations). *Contractor:* Bud B. Bollinger Construction Company.

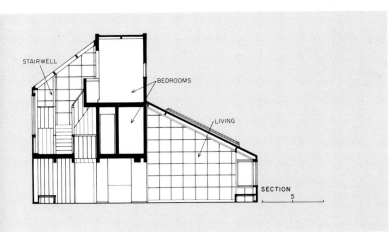

STAIRWELL
BEDROOMS
LIVING
SECTION
5

Morley Baer photos

Aside from the sun-filled living room (below left), the most dramatic space in the house is the staircase. Required by local codes, the double stair to the third floor has become a festival of forms lit by a translucent roof and a large window looking into the trees. Extra-deep studs with horizontal braces, all 2 by 8s, are used here and in the living room to create an interesting wall pattern and to provide vast amounts of book storage for the well-read family. The girls' bunk room on the third floor and the kitchen on the first (left) are both located in the "sleeping machine."

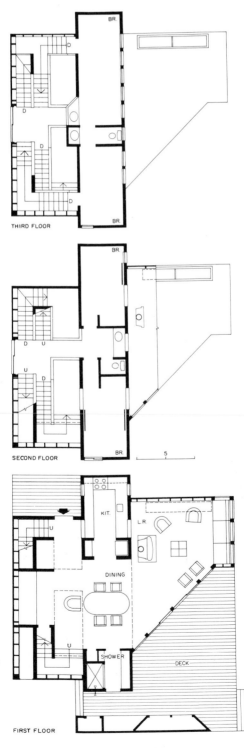

THIRD FLOOR

SECOND FLOOR

5

FIRST FLOOR

Seven lakeside houses

1:

The site: Crane Island in Puget Sound's San Juan Island Group. The architect and owner: Wendell Lovett. His program: a small, low-maintenance vacation retreat for his own family that would provide a holiday atmosphere and a complete change from urban routine.

The resulting structure is only 12 feet wide and contains just 370 square feet of enclosed space including a small sleeping loft reached from inside by a simple ladder-stair. Inverted bow-string trusses support the roof and suspend the deck that cantilevers 18 feet over the foundations. Within this structure, Lovett has fitted a compact kitchen, plumbing essentials, minimum storage and space for sitting and sleeping six. All furniture is built-in. The level of the deck drops one step (the depth of the joists—see section) inside to accommodate the mattress seating.

Much of the fun of this house comes from the boldness of the concept: the tightness of the plan contrasted against the audacity of the long cantilever, as well as from the skill with which the house exploits the site and view. The detailing is neat and clean throughout but never fussy, and retains a very pleasant and appropriate sense of informality.

In form and color, the interiors carry through the design theme stated so simply and forcefully on the exteriors. There is no wasted motion in the design and hardly a space or element that is not put to multiple use. Of all the houses in this collection, perhaps none is conceived and executed with more singleness of purpose or realizes its design goals more completely.

All structural lumber is Douglas fir. Exterior and interior cladding is rough sawn cedar stained to match the bark of surrounding trees. Cost of construction was approximately $15,000. A beautiful site; a challenging program; a neat and imaginative solution.

LOVETT VACATION HOUSE, Crane Island, Washington. Architect: *Wendell Lovett.* Structural engineer: *Robert Albrecht.* Contractor, *architect with Clifford I. Hooper.*

Christian Staub photos

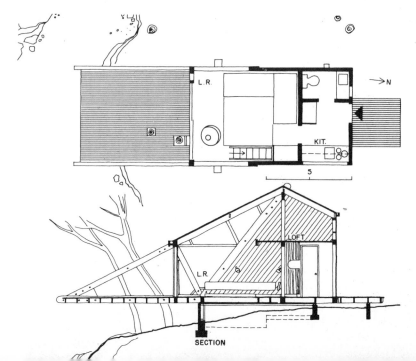

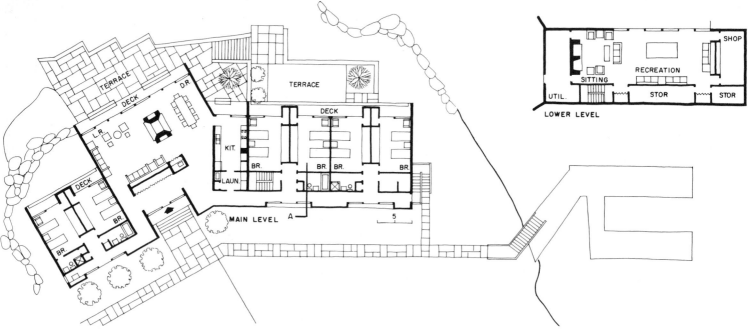

TERRACE

TERRACE

DECK

D.R.

DECK

L.R.

KIT.

BR.

BR. BR.

BR.

DECK

LAUN.

BR.

BR.

MAIN LEVEL   A   5

SHOP

RECREATION

SITTING

UTIL.   STOR   STOR

LOWER LEVEL

2: This country estate was designed to accommodate with equal ease its owners and various combinations of married children, grandchildren and friends for both short summer weekends and extended vacation stays.

Located on a promontory overlooking New York's Lake George, the site is a difficult but beautiful one, with an unencumbered, secluded, and panoramic view the full depth of the lake.

The lake, or private, side of the house, toward which all main living spaces, including bedrooms, are exposed, open with glass walls to decks and spacious but controlled terraces cascading down the hill. The entry side (photo, above) is, by contrast, closed—deliberately withholding the visitor from full exposure to the view.

The quite large house is built directly on the foundations of the owners' previous,

1½-foot-deep, modeled reveals of windows below the clerestories form gallery alcoves for the display of the owners' works of art. Difficult soil conditions limited development of a lower level to the children's wing (right). Stepped-out terraces (below) relate this to the adult living complex above. Overhang in foreground is a bedroom deck. The complex as a whole offers approaching visitor a deliberate and varied progression of spaces, ranging from the grassed entry court, and entry to the opened up living rooms and decks and finally the expansive sharp-ledged terraces overlooking the lake.

smaller house, which had been destroyed by fire, since building a new foundation would have meant extensive rock blasting and removal from the site. By turning to advantage the oblique angle formed by the existing foundation (see plan) and by cantilevering the main floor over it in both directions (see photo, lower right) the architect was able to gain the added living space required —and increase the drama of the nearly perfect view.

A plan composed of three zones was suggested by the site and organized to meet all the clients' needs. The major space, a central living-dining-kitchen complex (see photos, following page) is flanked by a wing for adult and children's bedrooms (six bedrooms were required), with a game room below giving onto a lower children's terrace. The result is in fact a two-in-one house: when the entire family is convened, the building functions as a complex. But the children's wing can easily be closed off, so the house never seems uncomfortably large when the owners are alone.

Materials—redwood siding inside and out, slate and hardwood floors—are rela-

Relaxed furniture groupings give scale to uncluttered space within an open living scheme. Dining room is in fact part of the single major living space. The fireplace is free-standing to stay clear of glassed expanse to permit the close relationship with outdoor deck and terrace (left). Dark walnut millwork contrasts with the rich warmth of redwood ceilings and walls. A typical bedroom right, gets its own private viewing deck, and clerestory lighting from the opposite wall.

Phokion Karas photos

tively maintenance free. The house is electric-heated, offering individual room controls and quick response for weekend use.

Nearly every room is endowed with a counterpart outdoors, with the principal deck and terrace off the living-dining complex shown

above. "Decks on the adult bedroom wing look into an intimate rock garden," comments architect Daland on the Worden house, "while those in the children's wing afford a dramatic view of the lake immediately below."

Polished slate floors, used in the adult living com-

plex as well as in the game room below, echo the use of bluestone for terraces and walks, and handsomely contrast with the natural fabric of the rough, wooded site. Oak is used for all other major floors. Fieldstone retaining walls for terraces repeat the use of stone indoors.

Floor-to-ceiling glass and open planning, as well as the careful siting and placement of rooms single-loaded-corridor style, bring much of the drama of the site indoors, and increase an all-pervasive relationship of visual—and functional—indoor / outdoor space. There are many

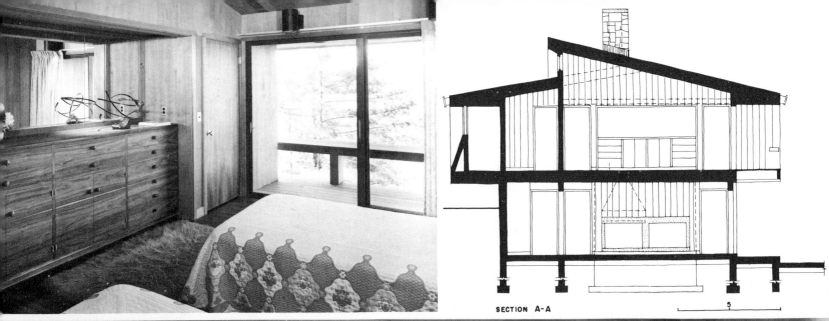

SECTION A-A

chances for seclusion from the view as well. Prominent clerestory windows form a major design motif and are provided to give each bedroom natural ventilation and a high, protected outlook amid surrounding trees.

Special outdoor lighting and built-in redwood seating

bring much of the relaxed vacation practicality and comfort of the interiors onto the spacious terraces and walks. Consistent use of beautifully detailed redwood siding for both ceiling and walls inside and out account for the expressively molded, sculptural quality of the

house, forcefully shaping spatial volume, while reinforcing the ridge-like contour of the site and providing a handsome culmination and focus for both the landward, grassed entry court and the lakeward wooded slopes and stepped-out terraces and walks.

Architect: ANDREW DALAND
210 South Street, Boston.
Owner: Mr. and Mrs. Robert E. Worden
Location: Pilot Knob, Lake George, New York
Landscape architect: Andrew Daland
Interior design: Andrew Daland
Contractor: Alger Mason

Norman McGrath photos

3:

A cool secluded pond is the focus for this house in the Green Mountains of Vermont. Access by car is possible only at a level 35 feet above the water, and so the entrance is at the top and the house is a series of terraced rooms facing the view and arranged around a central stairway that steps down inexorably from the entrance to the pond below, and just before (for the less adventurous) to an open deck and swimming pool.

The site and the shape of the house are both similar to the year-round vacation house on the shores of Lake Michigan (page 86), but

here the architect has been ardently concerned with the careful ordering of rooms inside and their relation to each other, rather than with preparing a swooping profile to be enjoyed from outside. He, in fact, points out that "the house was meant to be lived in and on, and not to be viewed from across the pond."

Exigency as well as predilection controlled some of the decisions, too, for the house is made of standard 2 by 4 framing, with standard windows, doors, skylights, and commonly available sizes of plywood and sheetrock, installed

with a minimum of cutting. For all this good sense, though, the house makes a remarkable impression on the land.

The architect points out that he was trying to put standard parts together in other than standard ways. This, admittedly, is not a unique intention today, as anything that veers even a single degree from the standard can skew the construction budget out of all recognition. Here, though, the attempt has worked: the house is not standard, and certainly doesn't look standard.

The long stairway, covered over by a 57-foot skylight, is a criti-

cal element among the special qualities of the house. From the outside, it helps bring the separate rooms together to make a single shape, and from the inside it performs a similar function. Flooded with sunlight, it allows movement up and down and across it, and even provides a place—an interior garden in the center of the house—for temporary repose; or for catching a passing glimpse of the sky or the water below.

Architect: PETER L. GLUCK. *Owners:* Mr. and Mrs. B. Bookstaver. *Location:* Westminster, Vermont.

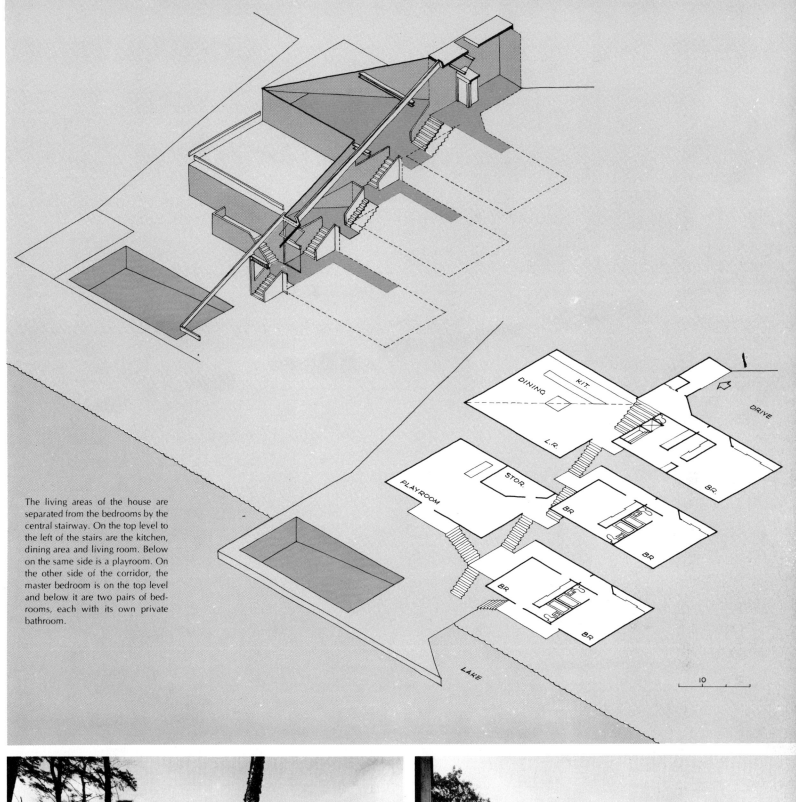

The living areas of the house are separated from the bedrooms by the central stairway. On the top level to the left of the stairs are the kitchen, dining area and living room. Below on the same side is a playroom. On the other side of the corridor, the master bedroom is on the top level and below it are two pairs of bedrooms, each with its own private bathroom.

DINING KIT

DRIVE

L.R.

BR.

PLAYROOM STOR.

BR

BR

BR

BR

LAKE

10

Near the entrance at the top of the house, the stairway opens directly into the living room (left), which is also seen on the right and above. The long skylight above the stairs allows solar heat generated in this space to rise to the top and exit through a large pivot window, creating a chimney effect. Outside air is drawn into the house from below, resulting in a natural air-conditioning system.

Photos: James Brett

4:

The client, Joseph P. Burke, hoping to build a weekend house on a low budget, had investigated builder and prefab houses before he engaged Rotner. Through strict economy of space and materials, the architect was able to keep the costs down to approximately $21 per square foot (1970-71) for a total of $34,000.

The house on a one-half-acre site in Watermill, Long Island overlooks a lake. Because of the high water table, only the garage is at grade. The utility room and first floor bedroom and bath are five steps up, the living room, terrace and kitchen are at midpoint and high enough for a view, and two additional bedrooms are at the top level, one of which overlooks the kitchen and serves as a study.

The three masonry walls of the garage carry most of the house. The floor joists of the kitchen and living room are laid on the two parallel bearing walls of the garage and the bedrooms are stacked vertically. As the section indicates, the kitchen and living rooms share a

12-foot ceiling. A secondary wall on the lake side (overleaf) serves as a *bris soleil* and frames the views. The principal entrance is inset and reached by a flight of stairs (opposite page, right). The window above lights the stairway and entrance hall.

Economies include a prefab chimney and fireplace, stock windows, conventional framing sheathed on the exterior and interior with one layer of grooved plywood and simple metal post and cable railings. Since the decks project over open space they didn't require flashing or waterproofing. Built-ins were done by carpenters on the site, rather than by cabinet shops. The single expensive item in the construction was the use of insulated glass throughout.

The Burke house was designed primarily for a bachelor. The two additional sleeping areas on the top level and the additional bath assures that it can go on the market as a family house.

Robert L. Rotner

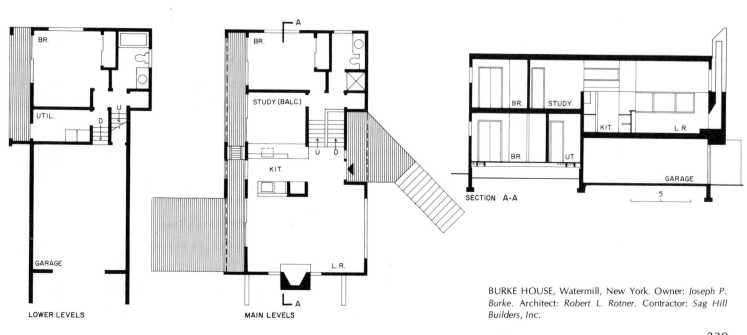

BR.

UTIL.

GARAGE

LOWER LEVELS

A

BR.

STUDY (BALC.)

KIT.

U D

L.R.

A

MAIN LEVELS

BR.   STUDY

BR.   KIT.   L.R.

UT.

GARAGE

SECTION   A-A

5

BURKE HOUSE, Watermill, New York. Owner: *Joseph P. Burke.* Architect: *Robert L. Rotner.* Contractor: *Sag Hill Builders, Inc.*

Architect Rotner has designed several vacation houses in eastern Long Island resort communities that not only cost considerably less than most architect-designed houses in the vicinity, but also less than many standardized contractor houses as well, proving that an architect-designed house can be synonymous with economy and value.

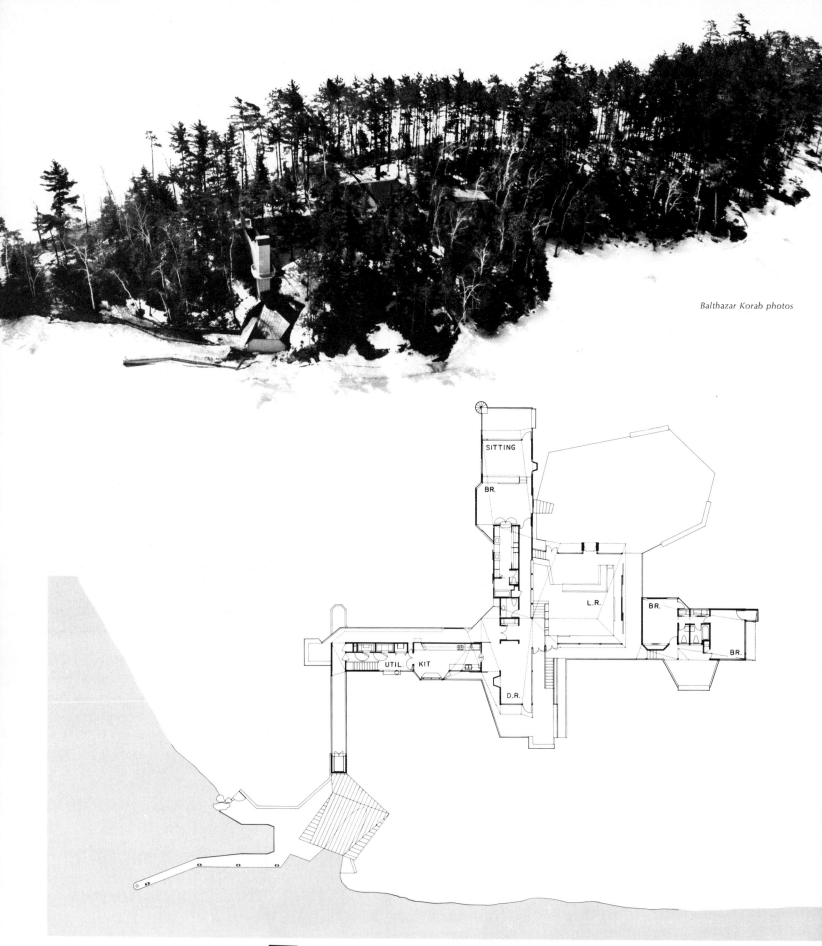

SITTING

BR.

L.R.

BR.

BR.

UTIL. KIT

D.R.

5: If you were to stand on the highest point of a rocky island and think about designing a house just for enjoyment of life and nature, you might design a house much like this one. It is a delight, full of surprises, and architect Harry Weese clearly designed it as a series of "why nots?".

Why not take people from the boat-house entrance to the level of the house by elevator? Why not let the house ramble so that every room opens on two sides to the summer breeze and view—and most have three exposures? Why not tuck little triangles of glass

into hallways so that even in transit from one part of the house to another one can enjoy the view of green trees against the sky?

The many-faceted roof might appear at first to be another of those "why nots"—but it is not. For it is a study of the roof that makes it per-

Aerial photograph and plan show the boat-house entrance to the house. An elevator in the foreground tower travels 35 feet to the main level, and bridges and decks lead past the kitchen and service area (with servants' quarters below) to the center of the plan—which opens to the dining area, the living area, and the master bedroom area. The guest quarters are set apart, at far right in plan. In the photo above, the living room is at the left, the long entryway to the master bedroom at the right. Photos left and right are the 30-foot-square living room.

fectly clear that there is—behind every element and detail of the house—a single essential idea: make the most of the site. In all of the rooms, the roof planes rise to carry the eye towards a view, and capture that view. Or the roof sweeps up to accent a space, descends when a space requires intimacy. That same concept applies in other planes—for example, in both the kitchen and the master bedroom suite, bays extend outward to create a new focus for a view. Broad decks open off the master bedroom (top in plan), the guest area (right in plan) and surround the dining area on three sides so that it becomes almost a pavilion. In contrast, the big living room (photo above) has a different spatial quality —protected under the biggest roof plane, shaded and sheltered by trees on one side and open to an enormous terrace on the "inland" side.

The construction of the house is wood, and much interior interest is generated by the exposed joists and the knee bracing (see livingroom photos above) reminiscent of Pennsylvania Dutch structures. Walls inside and out are vertical siding—redwood tongue and groove, flush

The master bedroom suite forms one wall of the biggest outdoor terrace. Photo left shows the living/study area with its own deck beyond; photo at right the view through the gallery back toward the center of the house.

joint, stained lichen green on the exterior; basswood, unfinished, inside. The roof is copper with standing seams —a material and form that emphasize the fascinating play of shapes and edges and ridges. The floors are maple. As the interior photos above show, all of the spaces are most varied, with many elements and details calling for attention. The master bedroom suite (lower photos, this page) offers views in three directions, a fireplace with glass above. The kitchen, opposite, offers work space under a tall bold roof, but a dining area set under a lower, more comfortable roof level. The dining area with broad decks, far right, is—as noted earlier—more a pavilion than a room.

Thus a rare house—experimental, perhaps arbitrary, but always thoughtful and responsive to where it is and how it will be used.

Architect: HARRY WEESE of Harry Weese & Associates
10 West Hubbard Street, Chicago
George Buchan, Toronto, associate architect
Location: Canada
Landscape architect: Harry Weese & Associates
Interior design: Design Unit
Contractor: Milton Goltz

The dining pavilion, photo above, is surrounded on three sides by broad decks. At left, the kitchen with its own dining table.

6:

For a lakefront site that few readers will identify as Fremont, Nebraska, architects Bahr Hanna Vermeer & Haecker designed an unusual summer house using cedar recycled from an old sheep barn for decking and for all horizontal structural members.

To assure privacy from the street and from neighbors, the house has minimal window openings on three sides. All large glazed areas face the deck and the lake beyond. The dominant visual element on the lake side of the house is a deep, wood truss, used to stiffen the entire frame and to give spatial definition to important outdoor spaces—an open deck and screened porch.

The arrangement of indoor living areas is linear across the width of the site with sleeping areas—including closet-top guest bunks—confined to the second floor. A split-level entry stair links the two levels. An outdoor stair, just off the master bedroom, connects upper and lower decks.

In spite of its comparatively uncomplicated plan, the Brandzel house masses strongly and differently on every elevation. Wood forms are used boldly in simple but expressive blocks and planes which are finished in cedar siding laid up in alternating diagonal patterns—patterns repeated on the interiors in floor and wall finishes.

Constructed at just under $20 per square foot, the Brandzel residence makes a virtue of bold forms with plain vanilla details, and misses no opportunity to insist that living here should be relaxed and informal.

Its rather bold forms are in contrast with neighboring houses, but the somewhat featureless site seemed to demand a strong solution—a solution the architects worked with skill and sensitivity to provide.

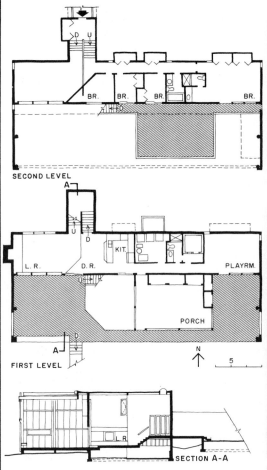

SECOND LEVEL

FIRST LEVEL

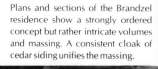

SECTION A-A

Plans and sections of the Brandzel residence show a strongly ordered concept but rather intricate volumes and massing. A consistent cloak of cedar siding unifies the massing.

Architects: Bahr Hanna Vermeer & Haecker Architects, Ltd.
535 Nebraska Savings Building Omaha, Nebraska
Owners: Mr. and Mrs. Thomas Brandzel
Location: Fremont, Nebraska
Engineers: Donald Thomsen (mechanical)
Contractor: Larsen & Jipp
Photographer: Gordon Peery

Marvelously different site conditions in three directions and dramatically varying atmospheric conditions, justify an unusual amount of formal contrast, one elevation to another, in this modest three-bedroom house. Light from a huge west-facing clerestory and from doors and windows on both sides of the main floor fills the living room all day long.

Mary Randlett photos

7:

Where foggy Northwest woods and the waters of Puget Sound meet, architect A. O. Bumgardner has created a romantic year-round vacation house. Responding to his client's memories of childhood summers in an earlier cottage on the same site, he has echoed the forms and techniques of indigenous residential frame construction. But also responding to the site's orientation to the east, he has opened up large areas of the roof with clerestories that pull in afternoon light in summer and during the mild but gray winters. Since no other houses are nearby, large glass areas on the main floor also open the interior to the outdoors. A huge cedar on the northeast side of the house and a fresh-water pond (left) behind the beach are two major elements of the site to which the form of the house reacts. Thus each elevation acknowledges its particular environment. Cedar shingles on walls and roof tie the composition together.

Location: Bainbridge Island, Washington. Owners: *Mr. and Mrs. Cappy Clarke;* architects: *The Bumgardner Partnership;* engineer: *Richard M. Stern* (mechanical); contractor: *Settle Construction Co.*

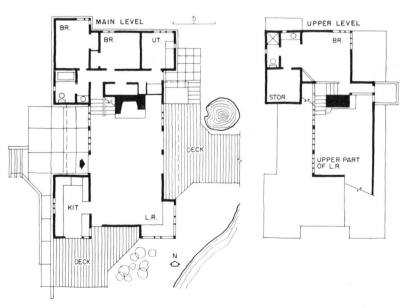

Index